FROM THE BOTTOM

A Ground Zero Approach to Community Wealth Building

TONYELL TOLIVER

Tonyell Toliver

Copyright © 2019 by Tonyell Toliver All rights reserved.
This book or any portion thereof may not be reproduced or used in any manner whatsoever without the express written permission of the publisher
except for the use of brief quotations in a book review.
Printed in the United States of America

First Printing, 2019
ISBN 978-1-7344803-0-6
Loves Greatest Story Publishing

This book is dedicated to all the people who are represented in broken communities all over the world.

The ones that want to come up out of their situations but just don't know how or where to start.

JUST START...

City to City

Hood to Hood

Ghetto to Ghetto

I HEAR YOU

To my grandmother, I Love You **Mrs. Mary**

Contents

INTRODUCTION .... **VIII**

CHAPTER 1

IF YOU ARE POOR; THE GOVERNMENT IS NOT YOUR FRIEND. 1
- GOVERNMENT TAXES REGULAR PEOPLE FIRST 4
- BEING POOR IS TOO EXPENSIVE 7
- POVERTY STATE IN AMERICA TODAY 8
- THE TWO KINDS OF POVERTY 13
- ESCAPING POVERTY ISN'T NEARLY AS EASY AS PEOPLE THINK 15
- BREAKING THE CYCLE OF POVERTY 18
- REFLECTIONS 24

CHAPTER 2 POVERTY IS NOT AN ACCIDENT. 25
- DO WHAT THE 9-99% ARE NOT DOING 35
- WHAT ONLY THE 1 PERCENT KNOWS 36
- STAY TUNED TO THE SECRETS OF WEALTH INFORMATION AND SUCCESS 41
- BE DELIBERATE ABOUT LEARNING THE UNIVERSAL LAW OF MONEY 45
- REFLECTIONS 48

CHAPTER 3

IF YOU DESIRE TO BE RICH, DON'T GO TO SCHOOL. 50
- THE MOST WATCHED TED TALK 57
- SCHOOL TRAINS US TO FAIL IN THE REAL WORLD 64
- UNSUITABLE LEARNING ENVIRONMENT FOR REAL WORLD 65
- LIFE REQUIRES WISDOM BUT SCHOOL DON'T OFFER IT 66
- SCHOOL GRADES DISTORTS PERCEPTION OF REALITY 67
- THE CASE WITH DEBT 71
- EDUCATION IS RELATIVELY INEXPENSIVE 73
- NO GUARANTEES 73
- FINDING PURPOSE ISN'T SURE 74
- YOU COULD BE LEFT FAR BEHIND 75
- REFLECTIONS 76

CHAPTER 4 YOU AND YOUR MIND 78
- Form Your Own Beliefs 85
- STEP 1: YOU MUST STATE A SPECIFIC BELIEF FIRST 87

STEP 2: HAMMER THAT BELIEF INTO YOURSELF REPEATEDLY AND CONTINUOUSLY.. 88
    Write It Down... 90
    Place It Everywhere You Can See It... 91
    Visualize That Your Belief Has Already Been Achieved Every Day 91
STEP 3: BE DETERMINED TO ASSOCIATE WITH THOSE WHO SHARE YOUR BELIEFS 93
STEP 4: YOU MUST CONFIRM YOUR BELIEF IN YOUR ENVIRONMENT 94
STEP 5: TAKE MASSIVE ACTION 95
STEP 6: ACKNOWLEDGES PROGRESS MADE 97
STEP 7: REPEAT, REPEAT, AND REPEAT 97
REFLECTIONS... 101

CHAPTER 5 TAKE THE RESPONSIBILITY 102

TAKE 100 PERCENT RESPONSIBILITY FOR YOUR LIFE 105
REFLECTIONS... 109

CHAPTER 6

INVEST IN YOURSELF 110

    Investing In Self Is the Secret of the Rich................................... 119
    How to Develop Personally.. 121
    You Hold the Key to Your Success... 124
    You Want to Become Rich? Do These Things 127
    Work To Learn, Not For Money 132
REFLECTIONS... 141

CHAPTER 7

UNDERSTANDING THE MONEY GAME... 142

    Make More Value, Not Money 151
REFLECTIONS... 167

REFERENCES.. 168

ABOUT THE AUTHOR 171

"everything you've ever wanted, is one step outside your comfort zone"

I take this opportunity to thank my mother who has been my rock/best friend/mentor and comedian when laughter was all I needed. Special thanks are due to Claire, for her continuous support and understanding, but also for committing to earlier versions of the book. My thanks are extended to my immediate family that live with me and had to put up with months of my isolation. Badu and WBSIW I Love You

I would like to acknowledge my indebtedness and render my warmest thanks to my soul brother/mentor, Patrick Young, who made this work worth doing. His friendly guidance and expert advice have been invaluable throughout all stages of the work.

I would also wish to express my gratitude to family and friends for extended discussions and valuable suggestions which have contributed greatly to the improvement of thinking outside the box and pulling out all my personal experiences.

The person with the greatest indirect contribution to this work is one of my professors. Thank you for teaching me the Singapore way of thinking and teaching.

Warmest thanks to my brother Ed, for being a father to me all those years. Trusting and guiding me through years of hardship. You are a true leader, father and family man.

Hurry home so we can continue American Dreaming.

INTRODUCTION

If poverty was a disease, then it would have a cure! The American Society is plagued with an ever-increasing demand for foods, shelters and income to make lives comfortable. The government reports that poverty levels are at an all-time low. In fact, the percentage of unemployment currently is less than 11.8% across the United States. That is not entirely true, nearly 40 million people are living in poverty and they rely on a system that will try to keep them poor. The truth is that the government keeps a certain number of the population poor to make public assistance "relevant" in some way. Well, if everyone was rich, what would individuals running for government offices actually campaign about? The system is designed to give the poor just enough to satisfy the barest basic need and anyone that is rich can live out their wildest dreams. Statistically, poor people pay more with rising inflation than rich people. Hence, poverty is quite expensive to manage, keeps you going around a circle – living from paycheck to paycheck, waiting patiently for your payday to come.

The reason is that your wages are heavily taxed so much that you live on an after taxed allowances (pocket change). This book is written to be an eye opener for you and guide you into understanding the schemes and plots behind poverty. But only you can break the chain of living an "average life". No one gets out of poverty by wishing for luck – well, people get lucky you might say but what percentage? 1% out of every 1000 people. That's a huge percentage gap and poverty continues to run repeatedly in a broken generational state not knowing what to do and how to go about it. Another reason why poverty seems generational is due to income inequality, the rich teach their younger generations their financial formula, while the poor can only teach what they know. The gap between the rich and the poor begins to widen as income inequality continues. People who work an average of 40 hours a week, really do not have anything to show for it. Very limited on living the type of life they dream about.

    Is poverty just a mere mindset thing? These are one of the most important questions we would be analyzing in this course. If poverty was a mindset limitation, I could wake up rich by altering my thought process, well it isn't that simple. Every successful person has a winning formula that works for them. They are people who have learned to understand what works for them and they have abided by it. The difference between the poor and rich is simply their "choice(s)". The choice they make at certain points in their lives is resulted to how they turn out to be. If you're poor now, it's important you look at the choices you've made and how they have affected you. You ought not to repeat the same patterns that made you poor. Successful people have trained themselves to master the art of excelling at what they do. Being successful doesn't mean you don't have setbacks. Each setback is a leeway for more opportunities to come.

Albert Einstein said, "We can't solve problems by using the same kind of thinking we used when we created them." Your thought process must change considerably to affect your life physically. The government will continue to make policies that seems helpful for every common citizen in the country but these policies are not for the poor people living on the edge to survive daily challenges. Only you can change your status quo by getting ready to make use of important details in this book. The rate of unemployment has not in any way decreased. The jobs lost during the recession are not in the same volume with respect to the current jobs available. Poverty levels are higher among the Blacks and Hispanics, and considerably lower in Whites in the United States. They make poverty sound like a "normal" thing, you begin to feel that you're not alone in it. It's the society's "rationale" that keeps so many people in their poor state. Poverty by association – a singular thought phenomenon that makes you think everyone is also struggling, you become complacent about the need to change your financial situation.

Poverty is not an accident, it's your responsibility to get yourself out of it. The statistics don't lie, people will continue to live in poverty because segregation would still be around, and racial profiling won't go away. School dropouts, homeless people, drug addicts, single parent working multiple jobs and many other individuals would keep on being poor. No one can keep you in your poor state, except you (you can reread that statement again). You're the way out of your problem, it's not by accident that you're poor, neither is it by accident that people are rich. There are paths you must follow, things you must do to develop yourself and get out of that miserable funk. You can continue to complain about your situation or what your local authorities are not doing to alleviate your needs and challenges. You can as well start planning for your grand escape into prosperity.

A state of laziness is surely a state of comfort, it's also of poverty. When you do nothing, nothing equally happens. It's like the ripple effect on the surface of a water, you throw in an object to get the effect. If you don't start planning, making moves and thinking about your future, you may never get out of being poor. Bill Gates saw the bigger picture when he dropped out of college to focus on his dreams, well I'm not telling you to drop out of college. The point is that you must have a direction and how to go about what you want. Poverty itself holds people down in a sense and makes them repeat the same mistakes their parents made. What you need is within you to help you develop the right frame of mind to harness your success. You may be born poor but it's your responsibility to become rich. You must prepare yourself with every opportunity necessary to become better, you must invest in yourself – your knowledge base must increase considerably.

CHAPTER 1

If You Are Poor:

The Government Is Not Your Friend.

> *"Tell me and I forget*
> *Teach me and I remember*
> *Involve me and I learn."*
> Benjamin Franklin

Thinking back to the 80s, some of us received our first lesson about money on television. One television show that comes to mind is the Cosby Show which according to TV Guide was the biggest hit in the 1980s. The show focuses on the Huxtable family, an upper middle-class African-American family with two successful, career-driven parents (the husband an obstetrician and wife an attorney) and four children (3 girls and a boy), living in a brownstone in Brooklyn Heights, New York. While the children had all going well for them with two career-driven and successful parents, they still had common problems relatable to regular kids who didn't have career driven parents.

In one of the episodes, *September 20, 1984,* Cliff the father and Theo the son were having a conversation in his room about moving out and getting a job like regular people using monopoly money.

Theo was happy making $250 a week. It was as though he could just build his life around it conveniently. Cliff gave him $300 a week instead, which amounts to $1200 a month. Cliff then took off top $350 for taxes. *"Government comes for regular people first,"* he said to Theo. Theo still felt he could still make something out of the remaining after tax. Cliff went further and after breaking down things Theo would need just to take care of basic needs, he had nothing left over for the rest of the month.

Theo had absolutely nothing left.

The wisdom in this episode unearth a great lesson about money and the mentality that makes people end up rich or poor in their lifetime.

The episode, I suppose, was meant to mirror to the society a certain mentality that kept people behind and poor in life in the 80s. But here we are in 2020 and it's still the same story for so many people in today's America. The Theo generation are still very much around, believing that being regular will help them survive today.

But that is a great lie. The government comes for the regular people first. If you think you can survive in America today by being just a regular person, you are in for a rough ride. It's either you are rich or you are poor because the government treats you differently. If you think all it takes to survive is to get a job with a good salary to take care of yourself and your family, you are never going to be rich because the system is designed to make you stay just like that—poor—and never get out of the trap.

From the Bottom

Do you know that Billionaire investor Warren Buffet pointed out that his secretary pays a higher percentage in taxes than himself despite the billions of incomes he enjoys? I bet you that the same is the case for wealthy people out there especially entrepreneurs who provide solutions and services for the benefits of the society and get paid handsomely for it. If the system is designed to trap the poor why would you ever be comfortable with staying poor and not reaching for your dreams? Why would the end of your dreams be to make enough just to serve yourself and your little family?

See, every state and local tax system, from Alaska to Wyoming, is inherently unfair to the poor. The poor always pay a higher percentage of income in taxes. According to a new study by The Progressive Research Organization Institute on Taxation and Economic Policy, the lower one's income is, the higher the effective state and local tax rate. When you combine all state and local income, property, sales and excise taxes that Americans pay, the nationwide average by income group are 10.9 percent for the poorest 20 percent, 9.4 percent for the middle 20 percent and 5.4 percent for the top 1 percent.

It simply means, the richer you are the lesser you pay in tax.

The poorer you are the swifter government comes to take their share of your pay. *Did you see that stat well?*

The tax is 5.4 percent for those in the top 1 percent. You see why you can't afford to have a Theo's mentality? You see why many people in America today ought to be deliberate about leaving Theo's camp and crossing over to the camp of the top 1 percent.

The government always come for Theo's camp first!

According to the study, in America today and in the 10 states with the most regressive tax structures, the bottom *20 percent pay up to seven times as much of their income in combined taxes as their wealthy counterparts.* Washington State is the most regressive, taxing its poorest residents at 16.8 percent while taxing the top 1 percent at only 2.4 percent. Other states with the most regressive systems are Florida, Texas, South Dakota, Illinois, Pennsylvania, Tennessee, Arizona, Kansas and Indiana.

Government Taxes Regular People First

I sincerely don't believe there's a simple formula to becoming wealthy. At least not beyond winning a lottery, robbing a bank, marrying someone rich, or inheriting money from your parents. While I may not be able to tell you a *"one way only"* to become wealthy, I can sure tell you one of the reasons the rich stays rich and the poor stays poor.

Tax is one of the most obvious reasons and I don't think I need any *"Panama Papers"* to bring that to light. It is the reason Billionaire investor Warren Buffet pays less in tax than his secretary who earns probably some few hundred to thousand bucks monthly.

If you are poor, the system—especially the tax system—is designed to keep you that way. The government is not your friend.

The system is rigged against you and if you don't know this you might never get out of the poverty trap. This is why you can't afford to have just a *"regular people's mentality"* thinking you'll survive this present society. *No, you won't.* Things won't get any better, until you decide to get better and beat the system that is inherently rigged against you. You think the government should probably have pity on you because your income is low and you aren't probably raking in millions yearly? Or you probably think the government should increase the tax on the rich and use the money to help the poor?

Let me announce to you now, *The government won't.* The system is designed to come for regular, poor people first. So, if you are poor, the only way out is to concentrate on yourself and beat the poverty trap by crossing over to the other side of those who are creating solutions and providing services for humanity and getting paid for it.

When being regular, you are taxed first and you'll also pay more than others because you only work for yourself *(salary)*. Government gives no tax breaks for anyone that only work for themselves and their families. As you can see from the stats that I shared earlier, only the wealthy who provide solutions and services that benefit the people get tax breaks.

Rich people are the ones the government comes for last!

So, why do you think Warren Buffet pays less tax than his secretary despite the billions of incomes he enjoys?

It is because the tax code works to the advantage of the rich in a few ways. That's why you have to break the poverty cycle and create wealth for yourself.

How does the government come for regular people first?

First, in America and many other climes in the world, taxes on labor *(salary)* are typically much higher than income on capital gains *(investments).*

The rich depend on investments. The poor and regular people depend on salaries.

The rich never work for salary. They know that the number of hours they can work within any given period is limited. Rather than focus on their labor like regular people do, they focus on investing and growing assets which don't require their involvement all the time. Examples are incomes they get from dividends, royalties, rentals, among others. These are incomes that keep pouring in without any additional effort unlike regular people that often substitute their physical presence and time for money. The rich map out multiple independent sources of income. This helps them to survive financial shocks and disasters unlike regular people who have nothing to turn to when their jobs are taken away from them.

Secondly, apart from the fact that government taxes labor income *(salary)* first, the tax code of America as a country is very complex. It is so complex that poor people don't just get to see it plainly that the tax system is rigged against them.

The rich have enough financial power to hire fiscal experts who will help them identify and exploit loopholes, litigate with tax authorities, and even move money into separate offshore tax havens if need be. They have enough to maximize all available tax exemption opportunities.

This is why a US tycoon can file for bankruptcy many times and yet keeps flying first class all over the world, while poor people can lose all their savings in a *Get Rich Quick Scheme* and never recover again.

Regular people don't have the time, money, or knowledge to use the seemingly complex tax code to their benefit.

Being Poor Is Too Expensive

The system is rigged against you, and the government is not your friend if you are poor. It is very expensive to not be rich in America today because after been taxed the first and most, the government still has a way of collecting the rest from you!

The poor always pay more to get or do the same thing as the rich. Do you know that poor people who don't have bank accounts pay 8 percent to cash a check?

According to a study conducted by the University of Michigan, do you know that poor people pay 5.9 percent more per sheet of toilet paper than the rest of the society?

The study focused on toilet paper because it is something that everyone has to buy and something that you don't use more of just because you have it on hand. Poor people cannot afford to buy it in bulk which is always cheaper because they don't always have savings and are often left with only a small amount to spend each week. Even when there are cheap offers around, it is also not easy to stock up because many poor people live in small housing where every square inch counts.

It is not just about toilet papers. The poor always pay more for food, clothing, housing, among many other things.

Poverty State in America Today

Poverty is a serious problem rooted in the American fabric. As it stands, more than 12.3 percent of the population live below the federal poverty line.

Do you know what that means? That's roughly 40 million people *(the entire population of California)* who are not sure if they'll have a warm meal or safe place to sleep tonight.

Yet, according to the Global Wealth Report, the total wealth per adult in the United States has grown every year since 2008. Welcomingly, the United States also sits atop the list of countries in the world with $98 trillion—the richest in the world.

Come to think of it, when you have a country where the average income seems to increase statistically yet poverty persists, you know something is broken somewhere. The Census Bureau says poverty has dropped since 2013, but in reality, the 2017 poverty rate of 12.3 percent of the whole American population is really not different from the rate in 1970.

Why am I talking about these stats?

It is because this cyclic pattern of *"macro"* national poverty is nothing but a clear reflection of the *"micro"* household poverty experience of the family home which for me is far more personal and trembling than clean graphs and sterile statistics.

The gap is getting wider than ever. Children born into homes of poor parents are finding it more difficult than ever to compete and make it in life. At the height of the recession in 2012, nearly one in four American children were living in poverty. Five years later, in 2017, America went through the worst economic crisis since the Great Depression and children remain the one still more likely to live in poverty than adults. The problem is particularly acute for children of color. While white children experience poverty at a rate of 11 percent, around 27 percent of Hispanic children, 31 percent of black children and 34 percent of Native American children in America today are growing up poor.

Many of these children are trying to get out of the ghetto and shoot for the moon *(rise above their background, neighborhood, and communities of underdeveloped environments)*. *"Trying"* is the word, whether in a legit way or not, but there seems to always be a big wall between them and moon! If you have watched the movie *"Back to the Future Part II"* you'll understand what I'm saying here far better. In the movie, old Biff of the future went back to the past and gave himself, young Biff, an almanac that contains all the winning sports scores for the next 50 years. That gave the young Biff the ability to instantly become a millionaire. All he had to do was listen to old Biff, bet on the game and collect his money. Question is, if this happened to you, would you really listen to your older self?

This is exactly the situation as we have it today in America. The rich, like the old Biff keep on with their legacy of wealth and social supremacy by handling down the lessons of wealth creation to their children while children born into poor and underprivileged neighborhoods are also handed life codes that further surround them in the poverty cycle.

Poverty is a serious thing. It is not just about money. If money is the issue then having it should solve the problem. Poverty rather is a mentality, a state of mind, and a pattern. It is what makes a man from a poor background sell drugs to make some money and the one who attained fame through his talents resorts to crack to maintain some form of sanity. It's a horrible world to be. Being born and raised in a disadvantaged neighborhood and community to poor parents *(who almost certainly had poor parents too)* has been proven to be a major setback in life. It's like the weight of heavy milestone hanged around the neck of its victims and plunged into the deep.

Let me roll out some stat so that you'll see what poverty looks like and what it feels to be born to poor parents who had lived all their lives in an underdeveloped neighborhood:

According to a study by the National center for Children in Poverty at Columbia University in 2009, researchers found that children who grew up poor were not only more likely to experience poverty as adults, but that the likelihood of being poor in adulthood went up with the number of years spent in poverty as a child.

According to a 2017 report from the Urban Institute, researchers found that 62 percent of children who spent at least half their childhoods in poverty went on to attain a high school diploma by age 20. By comparison, that number was 90 percent for those who never experienced poverty. Another report from the Urban Institute in 2015 showed that 23 percent of children who spent at least half their childhood in poverty enrolled in postsecondary education by age 25, compared to 70 percent of children who were never poor.

According to the American Academy of Pediatrics, children growing up poor are more likely to be injured in accidents, and five times more likely to die due to accidents.

Research shows that children who grow up in poverty are also more likely to develop chronic illnesses such as asthma or obesity—the latter can lead to further health problems, including diabetes and heart disease. Poor children are also more likely to be sedentary and exposed to tobacco, which in turn may increase the risk of heart and lung problems when they grow up.

Black adults who escape poverty are more likely to backslide at some point in their lives, in large part due to the other oppressions that plague historically black neighborhoods.

Poverty is unique for everyone. Each person's story may be similar but is unlike the rest. This is more the reason why quota-assessed programs and theories based on numbers instead of people always fail to produce a lasting transformation for individuals and families rooted in poverty. It only brings about a temporary relief. Let me share an example with you.

In 2005, the National Institute of Justice shared a devastating study of incarcerated individuals in 30 states. The release reads: *"Within five years of release, about three-quarters (76.6 percent) of released prisoners were rearrested."*

You see, those are the ones that left the ghetto, but the ghetto never left them. Those are the ones trying to shoot for the moon but end up crashing shortly after launch.

As long as we fail to create solutions that create a long-term result, nothing will ever change. The solution America needs are those that will empower each individual to realize and tap into their own unique gifts and talents, leverage on their unique experiences to break down their individual barriers and climb above poverty. This is how to solve the generational cycle of poverty. I'll share more about this later in this book because that's the heart of this project.

The pathway to poverty is grim as well as predictable. An individual grows up in an absent, irresponsible, or abusive home where the sight of food on the table is rare and no kind of attention is given. To cope with such experiences and find some sort of self-worth, the individual start experimenting with drugs, alcohol, and sex at a young age. They drop out of school. They fall further into an addiction, perhaps to harder substances. They can't keep a job. They struggle to meet basic needs for themselves and their families. Unable to afford rent, transportation, and/or food, their health plummets. They fall into crime. Incarcerated, they are damned to unemployment by a criminal record. They are stuck in a survival mindset, buried in poverty, with no way out. The future is bleak. Its either they circle back to crime or live a mean life, and most devastating to hear, pass the same pattern to their kids as parents.

The Two Kinds of Poverty

Yes, everyone's path into poverty is unique because our life experiences differs personally as humans. But even then, what places anyone in poverty can be grouped into two: situational or generational poverty.

Situation poverty is often caused by a sudden loss or crisis e.g. environmental disaster, domestic distress, job loss, addiction, or health problems. It's temporal in nature but if left unaddressed can enter prolonged periods. The second type of poverty is the generational one and this is the one I'm giving greater reference to in this book. It occurs in families where at least two generations have been born into poverty. It's not caused by a rapid event as in the case of situational poverty. Individuals and families who fall under this category often suffer psychological, behavioral, and physical barriers which leaves them unequipped with the tools to move out of their situations, rise above poverty, and do something meaningful with their lives.

You remember I wrote earlier that poverty is beyond lack of money. Yes. It is deeply psychological and behavioral as it sets individual and families up to consciously or unconsciously perpetuate the same cycle as their parents, repeat the same patterns, and eventually get the same results. For many people, the reason they are poor is as a result of a brutal combination of both situational and generational poverty.

One thing is very clear, and I want you to know this. No matter the kind of poverty an individual or family experiences whether its situational or generational, poverty is not just about being poor. It goes layers deeper. It's like a venomous cancer eating up individuals from the core, sapping them of the energy to uncover their unique gifts and potentials, and hindering them from becoming who they truly could be. This is the unseen force that keeps people stuck in the cycle and losing every ounce of energy to change their narratives for good. With time, it grows stealthily into loss of self-worth, then hopelessness.

When this internal conditioning which is layers of barrier on its own combines with societal barriers, what you see is a very complex and tangled web that epitomizes the poverty experience—unique for everyone, but universally challenging to solve. This is why we have failed as a nation when all we try to do is look at numbers and statistics and neglect the human approach to the individuals and families experiencing these barriers. No amount of funding will eradicate poverty because poverty isn't just about lack of money.

Escaping Poverty Isn't Nearly as Easy as People Think

Before *"The Wire"* made Baltimore Sun reporter David Simon famous in 1997, he had published a book called *"The Corner: A Year in the Life of an Inner-city Neighborhood."* The book was about an open-air drug market at West Fayette and Monroe Streets in Baltimore, and it painted, with graphical precision, a grim portrait of the urban ghetto and the people trapped there. Everyone hailed it as a wonderful piece of immersion journalism. As brilliant as David Simon's work was, it can't compare to what the phenomenal Karl Alexander did. Karl, a Johns Hopkins sociologist followed nearly 800 people from the neighborhoods surrounding Simon's corner since they started first grade in 1982. The report was their own version of *"The Corner"*, called *"The Long Shadow: Family Background, Disadvantaged Urban Youth and the Transition to Adulthood."* What they found was something very insightful.

Alexander had set out to look at how family influences the trajectory of a low-income child's life. Thirty years later, he was so sure that family determines almost everything, and that a child's fate is essentially fixed by how well off her parents were when she was born. Of the nearly 800 school kids he followed for 30 years, those who got a better start— because their parents were working or married—tended to stay better off, while the more disadvantaged stayed poor. Out of the original 800 public school children he started with, only 33 moved from low-income birth family to a high-income bracket by the time they neared 30.

Other shocking revelations are:

Only 4 percent of the low-income kids he met in 1982 had college degrees when he interviewed them at age 28, whereas 45 percent of the kids from higher-income backgrounds did.

Also, he discovered that at age 22, 89 percent of the white subjects who had dropped out of high school were working, compared with 40 percent of the black dropouts.

As grim as these stat looks, a part of it also offered some hope. Alexander stayed in touch with 18 out of a random sample of 22 African American through to 2005 when they had become adults. Out of the 18, 17 had been arrested and convicted of a crime at some time in their lives

(Seven of the interviews in 2005 were done in prisons.) On the flip side, a fair number of that group had also gone on to get post-secondary education of some sort, and nine were also working full time—two making more than $50,000 a year.

This, for me, is a clear indication that not everyone from the *"hood was doomed to a life of poverty and crime."* These young black men from *"The Corner"* were working steadily and drawing a decent paycheck. In all, you can see that escaping poverty isn't nearly as easy as people think it is.

When you think about Rick James saying *"something had a spell on me in the ghetto"* as far back as in one of his songs in the 80's, then you get the idea. It's a spell, a kind of inbuilt pattern hanging over your head until you produce the same result you've always seen around you. The implication is that where you started in life is where you are more likely to end up in life.

Please don't give in to all the *"American Dream"* paparazzi you see flying all around.

The American Dream is built on the notion that anyone can get ahead— that monetary security, financial comfort, and even the occasional vacation or luxury item are all within reach to any and all citizens. This deep-rooted belief is often reinforced by our upbringing *(we point to straight-from-the hood-to-fame stories of pops stars)* and the political view our leaders throw all around. The equation of success is something that is quite simple: *If you can work hard, you will get ahead in life*. Believing this means that we should accept that poverty is something we brought upon ourselves.

Unfortunately, this idea is so untrue and incorrect because it thrives on the assumption that the playing field is perfectly leveled—that we live in a society and an economic system that rewards hard work equally. While the idea that everyone can tap into various opportunities modern America provides one way or the other might seems true, the reality of the impoverished still remain that there are a variety of emotional, physical, and even neurological disadvantages that come along with childhood poverty. If you're born poor, there's only a 30% chance that you'll ascend to the middle class *(and this number drops significantly depending on your ethnicity)*. Once you're born poor in the US, you tend to stay there and raise your children there. Once you are born into poor households, the deck is really stacked against you.

How much money parents made remains one of the biggest indicators of a child's success, not how hard they work as an adult. Kids from the upper and middle class are more likely to make it out of college with a degree than those from low-income families regardless of their grades or performance. This is because, while generational poverty upsets the internal conditioning of poor kids, there are also the trappings of systemic poverty woven into the fabric of daily lives of individuals and families who live in economically depressed areas.

For children born into impoverished households, pieces of the poverty legacy start impacting their core from day one. It goes on to create a strong foundation that becomes very difficult to dismantle as they get older.

This foundation becomes a life template for them and forms their day to day living pattern. Many never get out of this cage until they are given the tools to do so and make meaning out of their lives. So, how do we break the poverty cycle?

Breaking the Cycle of Poverty

It's high time we started a conversation about how to break the cycle of poverty in America.

Poverty in America today might be easier to endure than it was 50 years ago, but it's not any easier to escape. To break the generational cycle of poverty, the answer we seek lies in looking beyond quick fixes and instant gratification. We must shift our focus to achieving long-term outcomes that go beyond the ability to endure poverty but rather how we can transform individuals' lives from that of surviving mode to thriving mode.

I'm not surprised by many of the countless, ineffective government programs out there claiming to tackle the issue of poverty in America. I personally believe that the system is created to make you stay poor so depending on it to get out of the poverty cycle is a great waste of time. Much private philanthropy out there only scratches the surface. You'll see all around ineffective programs failing to move people out of situational poverty, not to talk of the generational ones. Food stamps, band aids, among others that fosters dependency on the system and lacking no kind of long-term solution has been the order. For more than five decades solutions to poverty have focused almost exclusively on addressing the symptoms, providing access to material necessities like food, clothing, shelter, and healthcare. These people don't just get it. *Let me give you an illustration.*

Imagine you are a psychotherapist and you have a patient right in session suffering from serious emotional breakdown. The patient had even attempted suicide and is really in need of timely professional help. But here you are, the so-called expert trusted to take away the pain and help usher in some measure of sanity and serenity. Instead, you rubbed your hands over the patient's head, calmed him to a couch, and prepared for him a hot coffee to sooth his nerves. Then, as he took the coffee, you kept asking *"hope you are okay"* till he finished gulping hurriedly in a way that even scared you a bit. As soon as you picked the sound of the mug on the glass table, you said: *"Please get home, have positive thoughts, take a shower, do something relaxing, and you'll be fine."*

That was all you did, and you discharged the patient. Meanwhile, you were paid your fees for the session. Even though your warm courtesy is part of the whole parcel, you still haven't done anywhere near what you are supposed to do.

Let's say you know of such a psychotherapist in town and you have the power to revoke his/her certificate. I'm sure you'll do it with great pleasure. You'll be so sure that he/she is a disgrace to the profession and the general public, and as extreme as it may sound, some won't mind seeing this unprofessional and mean psychotherapist behind the bars for few months. As gory as imagining this scenario is, this is the exact template that shows what the government and many private organizations out there do in the name of dissolving poverty.

A young boy is clearly showing you he is emotionally troubled, can't keep his head straight, and resolved to crime to live, but all they can see is hunger, so they give him food. A young girl started having sex at a very young age, given to drugs, lost every shred of self-worth, and becomes so unsure about her place in this world, but all they see is healthcare, so they give her drugs. Youths in underdeveloped neighborhoods are lost into all kinds of addiction, getting arrested and rearrested, unable to get jobs because of their criminal history, and yet what they see is people in need of band aids.

Can you see how we have been treating symptoms and not the real problem? Even though the results aren't there, I don't deny that many of these efforts are from good intentions. One issue I have with these good-intentioned efforts is that they do not provide a way out of poverty but motivation to keep enduring it. But much more, you'll see that they do not, in anyway, acknowledge or cultivate the innate abilities and knowledge of those who are currently entrenched in the problem. They aren't, in any way, helping them discover fulfillment and meaning in their lives.

We cannot continue to treat mere symptoms. To break the cycle of poverty in America, we need to get to the roots and help people to remove their own barriers. The solution is in empowerment, not band aids and food stamps. There is something the rich and wealthy know that the poor don't know which keeps them hanging on a system that was never designed to make them rich and ensures the cycle of poverty is perpetuated. People born of impoverished parents into underprivileged environment and underdeveloped neighborhood need to be shown how they can recreate their life narratives, to understand and tap into their unique skills, and find the gifts/talents God has wired into their beings. When individuals are taught to begin to look inward and find solutions from within, they will be empowered to permanently break down barriers in their lives and in the lives of those around them. The greatest transformation you can help a human with is not in giving them food, clothing, or money. While those things are essential, the most important is to help them believe in themselves and see possibilities for themselves.

This is one of the most important things you'll learn from this book at the end of the day. I believe that a generation cannot transcend beyond her body of knowledge. Even though I know most impoverished people have become masters at enduring poverty and are comfortable in that state, I believe with the right information which brings about empowerment and enlightenment, the situation can be reversed for good. Once you know better, you not only do better, but become better as a person. The reason why people give up so fast is because they tend to look at how far they still have to go, instead of how far they have gone. There is always a process to it. You just have to follow it.

If we can find a way to unlock such masked potential and veiled gifts in people, it will spark massive transformation inside communities because as soon as some experience transformation for themselves and start finding their feet, they'll lead others to follow the process. This is not an easy task, but it is worth it. It is better than getting our kids rid of a wrong mindset that wants the fame and money but doesn't want to follow the process. Poverty will never be solved with top-down, sweeping solutions, but rather a focus on amplifying how individuals inside their own communities are solving problems. The solution to breaking the cycle of poverty lies in empowering all Americans with the education *(I mean what the rich knows, not schooling)*, tools, and community support they need to transform their own lives out of poverty and become self-sufficient.

When these internal barriers are broken, people begin to alter their life direction in a new way. When they realize their unique skills and talents, they start to identify how their experiences, habits and skills can add value to those around them, and that completely alters what they see as possible for their future.

Reflections

- What do you understand by "regular mentality?"
- The government is not your friend. Is that a statement you have always believed? If yes, what experience or occurrence prompted it?
- Why do governments come for regular people first?
- What did you personally learn from the conversation between Cliff and Theo as discussed in the chapter?
- Do you agree that poverty is a mentality?
- How much do you think your parent's financial history has impacted on your current financial reality as you read this chapter?
- How would you describe being born into or trapped in poverty from a personal point of view?
- If the government really wants to solve the problem of generational poverty, how do you think they should go about it and what do you think should be their focus points?
- The America dream and poverty. How do you explain their interplay?
- Why do you think people spend their lifetime enduring poverty instead of breaking free?
- How do we break the cycle of poverty in America today?

CHAPTER 2
Poverty Is Not an Accident.

"Success is not an accident. Sadly, failure is not an accident either. You succeed when you do what other successful people do, over and over, until these behaviors become a habit. Likewise, you fail if you don't do what successful people do."

Brian Tracy

What do you think is the difference between the rich and the poor? To suggest an answer to that question, let me reiterate again a story I already shared in the last chapter. It's about the film *"Back to the Future Part II"*. In the film, Old Biff of the future went back in time and gave himself, young Biff, an almanac containing all the winning scores for the next fifty years. With it, young Biff became an instant millionaire as all he had to do was stick to what Old Biff had given him and just collected his money.

Now, what do you think is the difference between young Biff and hundreds of others who entered the game with him? You'll say he had a sure plan that guaranteed his winning. And you are right about that. I'll like to say *"knowledge"* and not just *"plan"*. He knows something others do not know and that was the edge he had over them. From time immemorial, this has always been the difference between the rich and the poor—knowledge. When I say *"knowledge"*,

I do not mean your regular meaning of *merely knowing something*. No, that's not it. I'm talking about application. The true proof that you know anything is *what you have been able to do and achieve with it*.

There is something the rich know that the poor and middle class do not know. There is a way of thinking of the rich that the poor cannot access. Why is it that just 1 percent controls more than 96 percent of the wealth on this planet? There is something this 1 percent knows that the average poor man doesn't. There is something Oprah Winfrey knows and held on to that others in the hood don't just get. There is something Will Smith knows about himself that others can't catch up with. We live in a generation where our kids look at Hollywood stars from the hood and think they are just a whisker away from it. They look at superstars and celebrities, coveting the red carpets, cashing checks, and never understanding the value of the struggle and process. Yet, they spend their entire lives chasing shadows because they won't just go through the *"process." Only if they know that there is always a "process."*

Poor people get enthralled by the fame because they think its overnight. Smart people want to understand the process because they know it's important to know what a person has gone through to become who he/she is today.

When Jim Carrey was just a boy of 15, he quit school after his family had lost their home and had to live in a van. He was switching menial jobs to support his family. Fast forward to few years down the line, this small boy had discovered the hidden ability to make people happy and would go on to land infamous roles in films like *Dumb & Dumber, Ace Ventura,* and *In Living Color* which shot his net worth to over $150 million from nothing. Many people remember the world-famous Leonardo Di Caprio today especially for his dramatic roles in films like *Titanic* and *Taxi Driver*. But the amount of struggle he put in to land those roles and more today does not compare to what he has been through. He grew up *"very poor"* and was constantly surrounded by drugs and prostitution. Today, this same man has risen to become a globally celebrated Hollywood star that earns as much as $25 million for starring in a single movie!

A certain lady called Dolly grew up dirt poor. She was raised in a one room cabin in the woods with dirt floors and little money. Her parents, very poor, worked excruciatingly hard to the stretch of a dollar. We all know the story today. She is the same Dolly Parton that has reinvented country music all over the world today and sitting on a growing net worth of at least $500 million.

I'll be very surprised if you don't know Oprah Winfrey. Before becoming one of the richest self-made women in the world today, she had one of the roughest childhoods you can ever think of. Growing up in rural Mississippi on her very poor grandmother's farm, she then started moving around a lot until she eventually landed in a boarding home in Milwaukee. There, she was surrounded by extreme poverty and sexual assault in her father's house in Nashville, Tennessee. Distraught and seemingly hopeless, she dropped out of college early to pursue her dreams in media. Finding a solution inward and unleashing her gifts, she not only rose above extreme poverty *(she is worth more than 3 billion dollars)*, but has helped fan the embers of hope in the lives of millions of women all over the world who, through her story, believed in what is possible for them in life.

Would you believe that Howard Schultz, the popular chairman and CEO of Starbucks, watched his parents seriously struggle to make ends meet as a kid and was the first of his family to ever graduate from college? And there is Mark Wahlberg. He started out as a common street rat, frequently racking up petty crime allegations for stealing cars and drugs. He was the youngest of nine kids and came from a family where the most important lesson is how to live frugally. You know what? This same family that looked like *"bought into poverty"* has become entirely successful in their own right. The eldest brother, Paul Wahlberg, runs the highly acclaimed burger chain Wahlburgers. Mark, the youngest, has gone from rags to riches as a superstar actor, producer, and the mastermind behind hits such as Entourage, Ted, and Transformers. Donnie Wahlberg is another of the family that made his claim to fame as a member of the boy band, *New Kids on the Block*.

I can go on and on to mention names that you probably know—people that were born into a cycle of poverty and eventually turned out well in life, reaching their highest potentials, living their life purposes, and achieving their life dreams. One thing you'll see that's peculiar about these names I mentioned is that they reached into themselves, conjured the magic God has wrapped inside of them, dared to believe, shared their gifts/skills with the world, and in the process broke the chain of poverty.

Jim Carrey found inside of himself the gift to make people laugh and be happy. Leonardo Di Caprio and Mark Wahlberg discovered the superstar actor within themselves. Dolly Parton found her ingenious singing ability. Oprah discovered she was born and made for the screens. And many more. This is exactly what I would have you do after reading this book—to find that gift inside of you, share it with the world, and use it to rise above poverty.

Drugs, extreme poverty, hunger, homelessness, destitution, among others are horrible things in life that go a long way to reduce anyone's life options and place a certain embargo on how far they can go in life. For every Oprah, Mark, Leonardo, Jim, and others, there are thousands more like them that remained rooted in the cycle of poverty and never got out. Why is that? I think the answer isn't something complex. To break the cycle of poverty and cross over from the 96 percent to the 1 percent of this world, it demands a certain kind of mentality, belief system, core values, among others. I call this the *"process."* It is not instant. It is a process. Crossing to the other side isn't about accumulating money. It is about becoming a person that delivers value one way or the other to the world. And wherever value is been delivered, wealth naturally follows.

Breaking through, changing your narrative, and becoming a person that rises above poverty isn't about how much money you can accumulate. It is about developing the mindset of the rich and wealthy. It is about knowing what the 1 percent knows and has kept them in the cycle of wealth. It is about shattering every mindset that feeds poverty and lack. Without this mindset, nothing really changes no matter the amount of money on the outside. This is the reason we have people today that *are so poor that all they have is money*. I repeat *all they have is money, but they are poor*.

You see, a person that never held a millionaire dollars in his mind before might go crazy at receiving an alert of the same on his smartphone. If he suddenly enters his room and found a bail of dollar bills of the said amount heaped up on his bed, he'll probably run mad. Often times, such a person, after having this amount of money will naturally find a way to self-sabotage until he is back to his normal state—a state of extreme poverty. It's a way of his mind telling him he can't handle such amount. If the highest he has ever been used to is a thousand dollars, he will self-sabotage through all means to return to that state. Until his balance drops to a thousand dollars, he will be uncomfortable. He will throw cash around to prove some points to people that don't care about him. He will develop strange, money-wasting appetites. He will do everything and anything to let the money go until he reaches his comfort state again. I love the way the finance guru Robert Kiyosaki worded it when he wrote in one of his books that: *Rich people buy luxuries last while the poor and middle class tend to buy luxury first*. This is why you'll see many self-made millionaires out there affirm that *wealth and poverty are both habits*.

Ask anybody in America today that came right from a hood rimmed with extreme poverty and gross underdevelopment. They'll tell you that from time to time, people get chances and platforms that if maximized would put them on a trajectory to wealth and a life of impact. But the story is always that one way or the other the opportunity *"slipped"* as a result of self-sabotaging, impoverished habits.

If life is all about money you'll see lottery winners stay as millionaires for life. What do we see instead? They end up becoming miserable than they were before. Anytime windfall meets a poverty mindset the outcome is always something dangerous. This is same for those that got the *"big breaks"* from the hood and the instant fame became their greatest undoing. The poor chase money so hard in order to get it and never do. The rich rather, work on themselves to become a kind of person that attracts the amount they want in their lives *(you'll understand this much more later on)*. Somebody once said that if you take all the wealth in the world today and share it equally between all the people on the earth in less than 10 years, everything will start shaping up back to exactly how it is now: *1 percent owning the wealth of the remaining 96 percent.*

Why?

You see, many of the impoverished people always think that money is the problem, but that's incorrect. Giving them money is like pouring a drum of water into a basket. They are comfortable in that state mentally. Because money is mental and psychological, ten years after all the money has been shared equally, the ones that were rich before will find ways to attract more while the poor, through some forms of self-sabotage, will lose the money back so as to keep the 1 vs. 96 percent balance. This is one of the reasons why sometimes, the poorest people you see around are the hardest working people you'll ever meet. And the issue is, while they work hard for the money, there is an alarm in their head that triggers every form of self-sabotage which makes them eventually lose the same money they just had. This is why the rich don't get scammed by Pyramid and Get Rich Quick Schemes around, and the poor fall for it every now and then. Do a quick research on past lottery winners and it will all make perfect sense to you.

Too many people spend the money they haven't earned, to buy things they don't want, to impress people they don't like.

-Will Rogers

Many people in America today who are born into extreme poverty might never experience financial freedom because their parents never did. So, if you want financial freedom and want to live your life to the fullest, you'll have to adopt new teachers. You wouldn't expect your grandparents and parents to teach you something they have never experienced, which is financial freedom. If they knew better, they would have improved the quality of their own lives and changed their narratives. They couldn't. They not only felt stuck, they were really stuck. They couldn't even survive being poor.

Poverty and wealth are both habits. Poverty and wealth are both mindsets. Poverty and wealth are both belief systems. Poverty and wealth are both narratives we have told ourselves about ourselves repeatedly and has shaped our lives. Both poverty and wealth are about what you know and what you can do with that which you know.

A wise man once said: *"If you are born poor it isn't your fault, but if you die poor it's your fault."*

That is very true. It is your responsibility to break the cycle of poverty. It is your responsibility to find that *"missing step"* and understand the *"process"* it takes to find your purpose and live your life to its highest potential. It is your responsibility to seek for knowledge and know what the 1 percent of this world know what those who are wallowing in poverty don't know. It's your responsibility to start thinking like the rich and wealthy.

Yes, it is your responsibility.

If you don't want the cycle of poverty to keep repeating itself generations over generations, you'll agree with me that something different must happen and you are going to be the initiator of it. If you don't, nothing will ever change. It is your responsibility to create meaning out of your life and set the path right for the coming generation.

Are you getting ahead in life in any way? I want to believe that for you, and for many out there, the answer is more likely to be a big *"No"*. You are probably running from one job to the other or watching as your expenses rises and rises to trump your income and how everything seems to be crumbling around you. You feel stuck. You know firsthand what a rat race looks like. You know deep inside that your life is wasting away. You know you are just existing, and not living. Something inside of you, beyond bouts of depression and addictions that eats you up, keeps telling you that there is more to life. You agree, but you feel helpless.

So, what's your plan? I really don't know.

Relax. That is why we are both here right now.

What I can tell you boldly is that the government is not coming for you. The systems set up and put in place are actually meant to keep the poor just poor. It is to give just enough hand-outs to comfort the current mental state of mind *(enduring poverty and not escaping it)* of the impoverished. No organization is coming for you. Do you know why?

Only very few of the ones out there are actually serious. Others uses cosmetic approaches, treating the symptoms and not the cause. Food banks will alleviate your hunger but will hardly lead you to reaching inward and unleashing the gifts within you through which you can impact the world with in your own unique way.

Nobody is coming for you. Do you know why? We are inherently selfish, so expect that people will naturally seek their own interests first. Nobody will just walk up to you and say, *"hey guy, I really want you to end this poverty cycle of a thing." Your life is absolutely yours to take complete responsibility about.*

Only you can come for you. That is the fire I am stirring inside of you through this book. You have to stand up for yourself and make your life count. You have to start thinking differently and take actions differently. No matter how impoverished or hopeless you think you are right now, just imagine the examples I gave earlier *(Carrey, Oprah, Di Caprio, among others)* and you'll find out that there is an inspiration the world is waiting for in your story.

Do What the 9-99% Are Not Doing

Many people want to know the secret of becoming rich quickly. But they are not ready to pay the price. They are somehow, not ready to do what the 9-99% do on a consistent basis. They aren't ready for a whole new pedestal of thinking differently.

To break the cycle of poverty, become wealthy, and live the life of your dreams, you must act differently and do what the 1 percent do, first, by changing who you listen to and learn from. Remember: insanity is doing what you have always been doing and expecting a different result. That's the first lesson to start with.

Success is never an accident and that has been proven too many times. Success is deliberate and predictable because it has tested and proven principles that if followed leads to a life of wealth and utmost fulfilment. In the same vein, being poor and being wealthy isn't an accident. It is also intentional one way or the other. That's why you hear *"cycle of poverty"*. To *"stay"* in the cycle means you have a responsibility to follow some set rules which definitely keeps you there.

Often times, it is a step by step process to shape your mindsets mostly taught by your parents or society to become poor. For example, your parents or society will always say the words *"study hard, get a god grade, get a job, clear all your debts, and live happily ever after, before dying"*.

Implementing this statement is the first steps towards poverty. I devoted a whole chapter of this book to this absurd mentality which I believe is the reason many people in America are caught in the rat race today. We go on to implement several such statements taught by our parents or society and these speed up our process of becoming poor.

What makes a magnate different from you or me?

It's not in giving a million dollars to a charity organization or flying first class over the Antarctic.

It's basically the way they think.

Steve Siebold, author of *"How Rich People Think"*, spent nearly three decades interviewing the mega-wealthy and in the process found out something I have shared in this chapter already. The difference between them and the poor is that the latter think with a *"lottery"* mentality while the former *(that's the richest one percent of the population who own half the world's wealth)* think with an *"action"* mentality. So, if you want to add some more zeros to your bank balance *(or just keep on top of your rent and an online shopping addiction)*, it's time to adopt these habits and start thinking like the super-rich.

What Only The 1 Percent Know

To become successful in life and live the very life of your dreams, *to get to where you must be from where you currently are*, you will have to understand why the 1 percent rule the 96 percent. You will have to understand what the 1 percent know and do that the remaining majority are oblivious of.

Success is predictable. Wealth is a predictable result. Prosperity is a predictable result. I can really tell if you will get to where you must be from where you currently are. All I need to watch out for is your mindset, strength of belief, and attitude towards life and others. All those make being successful in life predictable. You can tell between two kids, the one that will end well and the *"otherwise"* one. Most people have been conditioned to believe that a person must be smart and educated to be highly successful in life and become wealthy. I challenge this belief for I have met and heard of many people who earn phenomenal amounts of money and have very little formal education. Do you know a guy call Bill Gates?

Just one percent of the population earn 96% of all the money being earned globally. While this statistic may be shocking and hard for some people to believe, it is true. It is the absolute reality. This small group of individuals employ some concepts to earn the majority of the world's currency. If you are poor, you surely don't know about it.

Bob Proctor, from award-winning film *"The Secret"* went from being a high school dropout to earning more than $100,000 dollars a year by applying the principles he learned from the book, *"Think and Grow Rich"* by Napoleon Hill. Bob never stopped studying the principles he learned from Hill's book and has been dedicated to helping others create lives of prosperity through his motivational teachings and trainings.

There are three strategies for creating enormous wealth and living the life of your dreams. The first strategy is used by 96% of the population. It's where you trade your time for money. That is what you are probably doing right now. This strategy has one major problem in that you run out of time. How much you get paid per hour doesn't really matter. When you see the middle class hopping on buses early in the morning in route to their job, that's what I'm talking about. Ninety-six out of 100 people use this strategy, and if they are able to save any money for the latter part of their life, they do it at the expense of living out their lives. They have to compromise on almost everything in their lives: *the house they live in, the car they drive, the quality of their apparels and accessories, the vacations they take, and the amount of time spent with loved ones and family.* With this method, I'm afraid to tell you, you can never become successful in life and live the life of your dreams. It's even good I say it: *That it is not in any way close to the highest possible life you can live.*

I always have the belief that there is more to life than just waking up, working, and paying bills. If that's all you do, you are merely existing, and not living.

But you really have to start living.

Another strategy, the second, used to create wealth is noteworthy and excellent, but is only used by about three percent of the population. It is a method that gave rise to the John Mark Templetons and Warren Buffets of this world. *It is investing money to earn to money.* This strategy is great if you have money to invest. If you don't have money to invest, it isn't.

The third strategy is the one used by the majority in the 1 percent category. There, you multiply your time by setting up Multiple Sources of Income that generates a constant flow of revenue, or you develop a unique idea into a product or service that is in demand by the masses.

The basic idea of this method is rooted in *"service"*. Great wealth comes through serving humanity with a service/product that is needed and in demand. Think of services like Facebook and Google and products like Starbucks and Kindle Books. I hope you got that!

Your service could be your gifts. It could be your well-honed skills. It could be anything you can offer to the world as *"Value"* and get paid for in exchange. We will get into that fully in the coming chapters.

Multiple sources of income creation is another aspect of wealth generation that works well for others in this category that don't have the *"big break"* product or services like Facebook and Starbucks. It is not also about adding another job to your list of things do. I guess nobody wants another job plus a job. It is about joining forces with people from all over the world, setting up joint ventures and setting up an avenue to bring in multiple sources of passive income. When you work on a global level, which can be easily accomplished thanks to the Internet and technology, earning money while you sleep is not only a possibility, but more than a reality.

If you want to belong to the 1 percent, you have work to do and principles to follow. Don't worry. It always works. Don't forget that success is predictable. Any principle that works for the greats can make you too great. Success principles are everywhere for the grab. Your imagination and mind will only take you as far as your beliefs permit them to go. If your mind is full of positive beliefs about money and your ability to create abundance, then most likely you'll get to be among the 1 percent one day.

Perhaps you are thinking that you just want a slice of the cake and not necessarily belong to the 1 percent.

Right?

Drop the pretense. Who does not want to be among the 1 percent? Who does not want to have great and resounding health and live happily in a gorgeous apartment? Who does not want a dream car? Who does not want to walk across the street and have people call him a blessing? Who does not want to have lots and lots of money? Who does not want to be among the 1 percent that control 96 percent of word's wealth?

Think about it.

Do you want to belong to the ranks of the 1 percent or the 96 percent? If your mind is riddled with beliefs and paradigms of lack and struggle in an area of life, especially about creating wealth— and you know it's something that will be a handicap— then the first step is to get your mindset working in harmony with your intentions, so you can achieve your dreams in life. When you do so, success in life becomes a no-brainer. What you believe is what you create in your life, and that includes money. Whatever your belief about money is, your ability to earn it, how much is freely available in the universe and how easy or hard it is to earn it, will determine how you move through and weather this current economic climate in America.

Stay Tuned to the Secrets of Wealth Information and Success

Now that you know you've got to change who you listen to if you will break out of poverty's cycle and create wealth, you have to be deliberate about staying tuned to the secrets of wealth information and success. Have you struggled for so long to find the secret to wealth that you're starting to believe you'll never achieve the life of your dreams?

But have you really dug enough? Have you dug out the right stuff? Many people claim they want to be wealthy, or at least financially independent. Yet most live from paycheck to paycheck and retire broke at the end of their lives.

How can this happen when there's so much wealth building information available in bookstores, courses, workshops and on the Internet? How can this be when we live in an era where there is arguably nothing that can't be dug out online? At every turn, there are range of books and subjects from financial planning, to investing in the stock market, real estate basics, and starting your own business.

There are thousands of audio programs, millions of YouTube videos, countless blog posts and articles, and hundreds of thousands of books that have been written on this topic of wealth information and how to achieve all-round success in life. However, one conclusion that can be gathered from the evidence these sources of empowering information provide is that: *There is absolutely NOTHING that is stopping you but YOUROWN SELF.* There's no shortage of strategies out there that can help make you amazingly wealthy within the next five to ten years.

The difference between those who are successful and those who are not, is not the amount of money that they started out with. It is not the education. It is not the connection or social standing. It is not any of the external factors. It is the ability to have complete TRUST in your own self, BELIEVE strongly in your own ideas without any apology, and ALLOW the success to freely come your way. You must learn how to attract abundance into your life. It is something anybody can learn.

Stay tuned to information about success and wealth. Invest in yourself. Buy books and audio programs. Condition your life the way it should be by soaking yourself in learning about how money works. Change your thinking and mindset. Try to produce the results you see around by learning from the principles that produced them. Someone said: *You don't have to be a wise man to get the result of a wise man; you only need to copy what a wise man does.*

If you must get to where you must be from where you currently are, you will have to follow the pathway. You have to take the bull of your life by the horn and assume 100% responsibility for why you are the way you are. You are definitely the reason you are poor. In the same way, you can become the reason you become se rich. Please if you can't get this right you can never become wealthy and successful.

The idea that someone is to blame for your circumstances is futile. It does not work, it never did, and it never will. Blaming others - be it your parents - for not giving you enough financial education will not change your situation. Blaming the government will not do ANYTHING good for you. If you keep blaming and pointing fingers, all you'll have is regrets and negative energy building up within you. Is that really what you want to keep doing for the rest of your magnificent life? Never! Accept responsibility and assume power over your life. You can do it!

To say there is nothing you can do concerning your circumstances is a complete lie. Everyone is capable of achieving that which they have come here to do on earth. There is a bestselling product in you. There is a bestselling service inside of you. There is a gift inside of you that the world is waiting for. You have absolutely no shred of excuse to not succeed in what you have come here to do, unless of course your journey does not involve success and freedom but suffering and pain. Why you may not ultimately join the rank of the 1% that controls the 96% of the world's wealth *(who's forcing you by the way)*, you must set out your life to become successful, achieve your big dreams, and fulfill your purpose in life.

Pay keen attention to wealth education and learn from the mentors *(those whose success stories you can identify with)* because energy flows in the direction of your attention. Whatever you focus your attention on is what it will deliver to you. If you sit there for example and fret that you don't have enough money to pay your different bills, the universe will work really hard to deprive you of any further income, because it thinks that this is precisely what you wish for. *The universe does not give you what you want, but what you pay attention to.*

Let me write that another way: *The universe does not give you what you want, but what you want so badly that you'll either have it or die.*

Please note this: If information were the only ingredient necessary for success, then all those people who take wealth creation courses and read books from Bob Proctor, Tony Robbins, Napoleon Hill, Norman Vincent Pearl, Joe Allen etc. would be very wealthy!

In the practical sense, the opposite is true. Only a very small percentage of students actually follow through on what they've learned. Why is that? Nothing really much, except mountains of excuses. But the real reason we don't utilize what we've learned is that we overlook the key ingredient for turning knowledge into action. To become wealthy, your motivation, habits, thoughts, self-image and emotions must all be aligned towards achieving that single goal.

Be Deliberate About Learning the Universal Law of Money

The road to utter failure is laced with the inactivity of those who choose to do nothing with their lives. You can choose to wish, daydream, and fantasize about your dream house, dream car, dream business, or dream anything.... if you do not back up your desires with solid actions then nothing will ever happen for you. The secret is this: *When your desire becomes an obsession; only then does your mind begin to conjure up all sorts of ideas for you to attain whatever it is that you want in life.*

Poverty Is Not an Accident.

I'm talking about a level where you want it badly enough.

Money and success answer only to action. There is no doubt about that. It answers to nothing else. From all corners of the world, one common thing about unsuccessful people is that they do everything in reverse. They desire to become wealthy. In fact, most would talk about becoming a millionaire. That isn't bad, but how will it be achieved? What needs to be done for that goal to be achieved?

Basically, wealth comes to individual as a bye-product of serving others. It is a universal law. This makes more than complete sense. You deliver value to other people and most of them will be glad to pay money to you in exchange for the services. How do you go about it if you want to become a millionaire? Find a way and concentrate first on the method that you will use to achieve it. Once that is settled, then you can wield all the forces in this world to apply specific actions needed in delivering your product or services.

You cannot do it the other way around and go against natural laws. Are you that clever? I don't think so. Take the focus off yourself and serve others with something they want and the wealth you desire will come to you aplenty. Common sense should tell you that there is an infinite greater chance of success if you align yourself with universal laws that have always worked for generations.

Anyone can have financial freedom. The laws are simple and within everyone's discovery. Anyone can enjoy increased life purpose, personal power, and prosperity if he can master the universal laws of abundance. *Poverty cannot stand anywhere the universal law of abundance is activated!*

Reflections

- In your own words, what is the difference between the rich and the poor?
- What do you think is the core reason 1 percent of the people control close to 99 percent of the wealth in this world?
- Do you think "fame" is a poisoned chalice? Justify your answer with a vivid example.
- Right now, think through your favorite celebrity or icon whose story of poverty to enormousness serves as an inspiration to you. What do you think you are presently not doing right? And what lesson do you think you can/ have learned that'll plant your feet in the path of wealth?
- What do you really understand by the word "process" as used all through this chapter?
- Some are so poor that all they have is money. Please attempt to demystify this statement according to your understanding of it in the chapter.
- Can you remember a point in time when you self-sabotaged (as used in the chapter) your way back to a state of lack because you had some "more" money? Name some of the wrong decisions you took, and maybe some strange habits developed during the time.
- Have you always thought the problem was money and all you needed was more of it to escape poverty and live the

life of your dreams? If yes, do you still think same after reading this chapter?
- To change your narrative, you need new teachers that will show you the way of the 99 percent. Have you identified some already? What steps will you take right now to take you further in the direction of learning from them?
- "It is your responsibility to break the cycle of poverty." What does that mean to you on a personal level?
- What do you understand as the difference between the rich's "action mentality" and the poor people's "lottery mentality?"
- Do an honest and critical assessment of your life in ten minutes.
- What do you think is keeping you poor? Why do you think you have not broken out of the poverty cycle? What can you do right now from what you've learned to get out?
- According to the chapter, there are three strategies for creating wealth. Which one are you currently using and that's keeping you poor? Which one do you think you should be determined to start using so as to join the 1 percent?
- Money answers to actions. What set of new actions have you decided to commit to after this chapter so that you can change your narrative?

CHAPTER 3

If You Desire to Be Rich, Don't Go To School.

It was in England, in the 1930s, and Gillian Lynne was just seven years old when her mother took her to the doctor because her school was sure she had a learning disorder. She was unable to sit still, always moving, and was nicknamed Wriggle Bottom. At age five, she already moved so much that her mother thought she had a serious disease. Gillian couldn't understand what was happening inside her slender, little body. She felt hopeless. Her teachers were exasperated, and her mother was at the end of her tether. She definitely had had it all, so she finally resolved to seek medical help.

Gillian's mother took her to the doctor. After listening to her explaining the teacher's concerns about Gillian's disruptive behavior and her own worries, the doctor and Gillian's mother stepped outside the office to speak privately. In the doctor's tiny office was a small radio and the doctor had put on some music before they stepped out. They sensed something was happening in the office. From the hallway outside, Mrs. Lynne and the doctor peered in and observed Gillian jumping and twirling around the room, enraptured in music, visibly energetic, and downright carried away.

How taken they both were!

The doctor turned to Mrs. Lynne and said, *"There is nothing wrong with your child. Your daughter is not sick. She is a dancer."* He then recommended she enroll her in a dance school instantly.

It was the moment Gillian Lynne became truly born.

Her mother did listen to the doctor's recommendations. She enrolled her in a dance school, and that was the moment her legend story started. *"Everyone was like me, they needed to move to be able to think. It was wonderful!"* Gillian said years later concerning her settling into the dance school.

By sixteen, in 1942, she started her professional career. Two years later, she joined the Sadler's Wells Ballet Company during World War II, and then quickly moved on to the Royal Ballet, which departed for the London Palladium. Fast forward about two decades after, she had already become a choreographic force. She became a leading and popular director and racked up credits for the Northern Ballet, Bolshoi Ballet and the Australian Ballet companies. She worked on many TV specials for superstar performers from a variety of musical genres, including the legendary Ray Charles, the famous Beatles drummer turned actor and musician Ringo Starr, fantastic television personality Perry Como, American singer and dancer Carol Channing, and multi award-winning actress Shelley Winters, among many others.

She went all the way to have a legendary career that brought her across theater impresario Andrew Lloyd Webber who is arguably the greatest music composer of our time, and she also later worked with the theatre director wizard Sir Trevor Nunn on the

Royal Shakespeare Company's productions of *'Once in a Lifetime'* and *'The Comedy of Errors'* both which turned out hugely successful and groundbreaking. Webber wrote that it was her collaboration with Trevor Nunn on these two projects that led to both their key roles in the creation of *'Cats'*. *'Cats'* and *'Phantom of the Opera'* would go on, till today, to be one of the most successful theater productions in history of mankind.

Gillian's extraordinary career proved naysayers wrong and her astounding success defied the odds. At the time she did *Cats*, British dancers who could also sing and act were few and far between and more so, the idea of a British musical with dance at its heart was unthinkable. She had to fall on her depth of contacts from her ballet roots to her work in contemporary dance in order to make it possible for *Cats* to be opened in Britain. It is no exaggeration that *'Cats'* opened with the only cast available who could have played their roles.

She directed over sixty productions in the West End and on Broadway, worked on more than 11 feature films and hundreds of television productions as an excellent producer, director, choreographer, and performer. Her ground-breaking staging and choreography for the iconic Cats earned her two Olivier Awards in 1981. She earned a BAFTA for her 1987 drama *"A Simple Man,"* which she directed for BBC TV. She also later earned a Moliere Award and the Queen Elizabeth II Coronation Award from the Royal Academy of Dance, which elected her vice president in

2012. Her overall contribution to the arts world –from classical ballet to feature dance performance– earned her a Lifetime Achievement Special Award at the 2013 Olivier Awards. In 2014, she was named a Commander of the Most Excellent Order of the British Empire from the Queen and made a dame for her services in dance and musical theaters globally.

The New London Theater, which was running Andrew Webber's *"School of Rock"* at the time, was renamed in her honor, changed to Gillian Lynne Theater, being the home of the original production of *Cats* which ran from 1981 to 2002 and was West End's longest running show at the time. It would be the first theater in London's theater district to be named after a woman. Gillian Lynne's groundbreaking work on *Cats* inspired and launched countless amazing careers in dance and music till today. She was renowned to fire people up with her own energy. She is the real definition of passion and hard work.

And not only has she given pleasure to millions all over the world, she actually died a multi-millionaire.

What do you make of the story of this amazing young woman who went from being a concern to everyone in her life, tagged *"wriggle bottom"* in her childhood, to conquering her world and rode at the very top of it? What do you think would have happened to thousands of potential dancers whom her life gave direction, people who might never have found their true calling and passion in life without her as a shining guide?

What do you make of the doctor's recommendation and her mother's resolve?

If Gillian Lynne was born today, what do you think would have become of her life? What would the mother have said, or the parents altogether? What would have happened if young Gillian Lynne grew up in our schools today?

Let me attempt an answer for the last question. She would surely have exasperated her teachers and parents just the same way she did then. But however, it is more likely that any medical help that she received would have resulted in testing, diagnosis, and medication.

She would have been forced to remain in school. She would have been talked and coerced into accepting schooling as probably the only option. She would have been condemned to living a life where teachers treat her as a medically-ill student—one with a learning disorder. I am in no way judging parents who would go this route. Not a bit. What I am suggesting is that we step back from our obstinate ideas about how things should be and ask ourselves how our expectations may be hindering our kids.

Somebody else might have put Gillian Lynne on medication and told her to calm down and force her into the traditional school system.

Somebody would have said to her: *you can't do without college*. Somebody would have made her understand that going to school, getting good grades, and doing something meaningful with a college degree is life's Holy Grail. Somebody might have pushed her deeper and deeper into a life of misery, and she would never have become the multimillionaire responsible for some of the most successful theater productions in history and composer of one of the highest grossing musicals of all time. She wouldn't have become the legendary Gillian Lynne we have all come to know today.

The story of Gillian Lynne is an example of something going right in a child's education. She was put in an environment that fits her skillset and stokes her passion. And few decades later, she's a legend in her field. In Gillian Lynne, it was the artistic ability to dance and her theatrical genius that developed over time. In Kanye West, it was all about dropping college to pursue fulfillment in music. In Mark Zuckerberg, Bill Gates, and Steve Jobs, it was all about leaving prestigiously renowned colleges to pursue their innovative tech dreams. In Oprah Winfrey and Ellen DeGeneres, it was all about leaving college to pursue their media dreams. Brad Pitt and Sylvester Stallone dropped out to pursue their acting dreams. The list is endless.

Type all these names into Google, including many others you know who did not take the college path and you will see how famous and hugely successful they have become in our world today. They have shown us that the road to success isn't one-way traffic. They have proven that success in life isn't about some certificates or professional papers. They have proven that, by dint of hard work and with the right belief systems, anyone can achieve his or her dreams. They have shown that everyone can create their path to riches and wealth. Through their stories and life experiences, we now know that there are 1 million and one ways to create wealth and make money without a college degree.

They have shown us that the entirety of what most people seek: money, fame, connections, comfort, authority, position, etc., can be achieved without ever stepping inside the barricading four walls of a traditional college.

The amazing success story of Gillian Lynne, and every other person in this world who have created their own stories isn't to say college or traditional education is a curse. Never! Rather, it is a challenge to the way we look at schooling in the grand scheme of our lives, and most importantly, our expectation for kids. We should ask ourselves: What does it mean to be educated? What are the goals of college education? What are our goals in educating our kids? Are we teaching them so that they can achieve goals that make us look good as parents? Are we sending them to schools because we feel it's their best chance at becoming something meaningful in life?

If you will hear the unpleasant truth, many children are not cut out for our school and colleges. Or are they? What about Gillian Lynne? What about all those college dropouts who have made a successful career in the field of arts, literature, business, social media, sports, online marketing, fashion and media, among others? What about those who continually failed, deemed as having learning difficulties, unable to compete in the school system, couldn't get around passing grade in most subjects, and are constant subject of derision from students and teachers alike, yet managed to become one of the world's most successful entrepreneurs? And how about college students from very humble backgrounds who leveraged on the power of the Internet and social media, selling things from their dormitories and making money that their class professors would probably never make in a lifetime?

Wouldn't you say that something must be wrong or missing in the educational system?

If you give these some serious thoughts, it will definitely make you wonder. You will wonder how come only a few excel at school, most make it through, more are below average in their overall performance, and those who were among the *"worst"* students soared high when released from the barricading four-walled corners of a classroom. It's really a magic.

The Most Watched TED Talk

Could you believe that the most watched TED speech ever was about how education kills creativity?

According to reports, the speech, watched on the TED website for over 34 million times and over 9 million more times on YouTube, caused many parents to pull their kids out of school and it was a matter of hot debate among experts. Ken Robinson, the man in the speech, is an expert on creativity and education and he strongly believes that, as things stand till date, the two concepts don't seem to coexist. Robinson argued in the speech eloquently and passionately that education is destroying our children's capacity to think outside the box.

I agree with Robinson. Not because of his achievement in the field of researching education and creativity. Of course, his achievements speak volumes. He led the British government's 1998 advisory committee on creative and cultural education, an inquiry into the significance of creativity in the educational system and the economy, and he was knighted in 2003 by Queen Elizabeth II for his achievements. Beyond all these, I agree because his views are just so right, and it's exactly all we see playing out right in front of our eyes today.

In the 19th century, there was nothing like public system of education. They all came into being to meet the needs of the industrial revolution. The idea and purpose was towards training and providing people who will be drivers of the Industrial Revolution economy.

At school, people are steered away from the subjects they love because they probably would never get a job doing it. It was all about jobs. Passions, interests, must revolve around jobs available in that era. If you were creative, brilliant, and talented, you'll think you are not because everything you were good at in school wasn't valued or would be stigmatized.

> *"All children have tremendous talent and we squander them pretty ruthlessly. I believe passionately that we don't grow into creativity, we grow out of it. We are educated out of it."*
>
> **- Ken Robinson**

Furthermore, Robinson believes that the society has a very limited definition of intelligence—one that looks at literacy and numeracy only. Students that cannot read and write fluently *(but may excel at other subjects)* are tagged *'not very bright.'* Those that wouldn't sit calmly, restless and seems disruptive, like choreographer Gillian Lynne, are termed as having *'learning disorders'*, stigmatized as hyperactive and diagnosed with ADHD. Our education system places so much emphasis on the academic subjects that natural gifts for art, music or acting are often brushed aside as we get older. The system rewards those who silently follow orders in reading and absorbing information while being slaved away in classwork and notes, seated at their desk. Few others who might have other ideas are termed as misfits. This is how our school system kills creativity.

Long ago, there were those who responded positively to unconventional schooling from the start. I am referring to the times when science was not as advanced as it is today and persons with ADHD were not properly diagnosed yet. Then, it took an unconventional approach from an educator, not a semblance of the rigid structure we have today, to make a successful child out of an animated, fidgeting child. If our school system keeps operating in a way that it is tailored to the conventional approach in teaching, then every college all over the world will produce robotic, one-way traffic individuals, who are satisfied with simple thinking to come up with a simple solution. We will never have individuals who can explore alternatives, engage in critical thinking, and seek to create massive solutions to deeper problems mitigating against our modern world. Where would the next generation go to if our schools will not be able to produce graduates with the ability to think creatively without fear of failure? It is no simple thinking to create a business out of an idea that seems intangible. It is no normal thinking to create an app that can assist in global warming and climate changes. It is no ordinary thinking to make lots and lots of money doing exactly the same thing millions have done and failed at. It is the power of creativity. It is the ability to unleash creative force within all of us to create something meaningful in life.

The whole purpose of public education throughout the world seems to be geared towards producing university professors. The most important metric used in grading excellence is academic ability. The best students are the one who come out on top. In short, we've been educated to become good workers, rather than creative thinkers. *Our parents, deceived by their own parents too, deceived us that going to school, getting good grades, and getting qualified for a lucrative job is as perfect as a carbon's cycle, that our college certificates is an automatic ticket to a life full of money and riches.* Colleges took over our lives, with professors sound academically but struggling financially. Sometimes, the idea is to step up into higher degrees, that it would mean being able to get paid higher at our workplaces or increase the chance of getting picked ahead of others for job opportunities. So, we pursue masters and doctorates, yet those who earn higher degrees, the so-called teachers and instructors-are struggling financially. And for few of them that feel a hundred thousand bucks as monthly salary is the next big news after Obama as US president, there are thousands of ordinary individuals under twenty years making more in less than a week from their businesses *(online or offline)* and living the life of their dreams.

When the idea of a business finally clicks then here comes the problem: Schools have taught us so much to live a reactionary life instead of a proactive one. We have been trained to study hard, work and get paid, and never to learn how to create our own money. We have become used to salary, studying the more to command a raise, while our innate creative ability erode away in the process. For those that finally remember that they have a passion for starting their own business, they start looking up to MBA to fill up the gap. Really? How many professors in business schools actually have a running business? The answer is close to zero. Isn't that really a shame!

Let me help you with a quick iteration of how our colleges have been killing creativity and I hope it will serve for you a go-to reference now and always in case you belong to that category where your parents seems to see school as the *best* or *only option* in life .

The creative element in a child is killed at an early age because most schools lack the motivational framework that can allow artistic and talented individuals to thrive. Students end up coming up with nothing of note from school apart from the drilled content offered by teachers. Music, woodwork, building and construction, arts, are subject that aren't given valid importance. They are electives. That simply means students **are not even encouraged to take or pursue subjects that** are in line with their talents and resident abilities. Imagine what would have happened to Gillian Lynne in today's world.

Students are constrained to conform to an ideology they don't actually relate to instead of being encouraged to have their own narrative and create something that will inspire their passion. And what do you make of the syllabus our colleges flaunt till date? Irrelevant is the word! The syllabi in play are not in any way relevant to the changing world setups. Students are been prepared for jobs that won't exist in the next ten years, probably taken over by machines and robots. Students are been trained for a world that no longer exist.

In our school system today, thinking outside-the-box is not rewarded. Those that think outside the box are been classified as being hyper and with active imaginations and having learning disorders.

The reward system of our schools is centered on students spilling out the factual content that has been provided by the teachers. Idealistic presentations are not encouraged. Students hardly have the license to expound or re-design the knowledge they have been able to grasp over time.

Free thinking is condemned in schools. Students are expected to consume without question. When free thinking is eliminated, students tend to be consumers of knowledge instead of revolutionaries who follow through with their creative ideas and provide solutions to problems besetting our race.

Our school system is all about rules and students who don't obey are punished. As much as there needs to be codes of conduct, punishing students for simply having other ideas means they are inhibited in terms of the freedom they have to make some decisions that are the fruit of critical and creative thinking.

Schools are run on a routine system and in such a system creativity fails to be an element that can thrive. Schools thrive on the idea that there is a routine that must be followed, and it is these structured systems that stunt creative development. But nothing great comes from following routines and doing things the same way. Albert Einstein calls it insanity, doing the same thing over and over again and expecting a different outcome. Breaking away from routine is what inspires creative thinking and development. Individual creativity of students is killed because schools operate an *"All under one roof"* setting. To ensure students stay creative, an individualistic approach where solutions and conducive environment is offered to each student is key. Without an environment where they can harness their passion and thinking, creativity can never be cultivated.

Schools only accept one answer as the correct one and every other solution or explanation is meant to be wrong. This means that students are psychologically tuned to have one answer and their ability to creatively and imaginatively seek alternatives is crushed.

School system stifles the expression of talents and inhibits creativity because the curricular isn't talent-based. The system isn't tuned to harness the talents that students have, rather it is aimed at instilling pre-selected material to the minds of the students.

Curiosity and imagination are considered as barriers and are met with condemnations because the school believes they are impediments to the systemic adoption of classroom knowledge. The notion impacted into students is that something is wrong in being creative and imaginative and everything is right with being 100 percent receptive to classroom knowledge.

School Trains Us to Fail In the Real World

Imagine if a medical doctor gave all of its patients the same medicine. The results will be catastrophic, yet this is what is happening all over the world with our education system. Students are educated the same way and no focus is on individuals. They give the same education to all the children even when they know each child has a different mindset. Students are made to sit nice and neat, put hands up before speaking, strive to get an A+, and eventually get trained to work in the factories and companies.

The school system was made for the past, not for the future. Let me show you in clear ways how schools have trained, and is still training exactly how to fail in the real world where it all matters:

Unsuitable Learning Environment For Real World

Some have the opinion that school is the place to impact wisdom to youngsters in preparing them for the workplace. If truly the school is to prepare us for a career, then why is it that it's absolutely horrible at accomplishing that? Take a look at these disturbing stats from a Mckinsey consulting firm report:

In 2011, 1.5 million, or 53.6% of college grads under age 25 were out of work or underemployed.

And for those that do have jobs? 48% of employed U.S. college grads are in jobs that require less than a four-year degree. 30% of college graduates don't feel college prepared them for the world of work.

Six times as many graduates are working in retail or hospitality as had originally been planned.

You see that? Before, apprenticeships were the norm as you'd learn the hands-on skills and expertise from a mature worker in your field. But scholastic education came and the mad rush to partake in something perceived superior began, only to realize that what we now have today is actually an inferior form of learning. Today, most professions need hands-on training and mentorship, even the digitally based ones. Everywhere today we see programming boot camps popping, and in 2 to 3 months 90 percent or more of graduates have a job making more than $80,000 a year, showing you how horrible the school model has become. Isn't that better than four years within the walls of a college and waiting for a job after graduation?

Life Requires Wisdom But School Don't Offer It

School teach kids how to cram and memorize information instead of learning critical life skills such as how to communicate, how to make, manage, and grow money, how to negotiate, how to make friends and keep them, among many others. There is nothing absolutely evil about memorizing, but not at the expense of life skills. I understand that many parents are not qualified to teach these skills because they are probably bad in it by themselves, so many assume that the school system would be the perfect place to learn these indispensable skills.

The truth is school has been terrible in this regard and kids are trained to live in a world that no longer exists. Please ask yourself, what good can a body of learning that lacks trainings in areas like finances, personal growth, communication, emotional intelligence, and healthy living, offer anyone? The reality is that colleges are not set up to teach what matters most. How about classes for important life skills like goal setting, habits, money management? How about knowing deeper things about money like smart credit card usage to avoid freaking 18% interest rates, how to build credit, how to pick the right health insurance, why new cars are a horrible investment, among many others.

School Grades Distorts Perception of Reality

Anyone can get straight 'A's in school but nobody, I repeat nobody, no matter how successful, gets straight 'A's in life. In school, you get an A to show you are just absolutely fine, but in real life, you tend to get lots and lots of 'F's before getting your A.

Remember Stephen King, one of the world's most successful authors in history? He still has his huge stack of publisher rejection slips. Those were *"real world 'F's."* Remember J.K Rowling who became the first female author that only dropped off the billionaire's list because she gave close to 200 million dollars to charity. She still releases, from time to time, her rejection slips, one telling her that no one in America reads children stories again. But you and I know what happened with her Harry Porter creations. Those rejections were her 'F's before she got her A. Successful blogger, author, and entrepreneur James Altucher lost about 17 out of his 20 businesses before becoming very successful with the few ones left worth millions of dollars. Colonel Sanders had 1,009 rejections he received for his chicken recipe before the first yes. And many of his rejections were *humiliating, as in, very humiliating—a flat F in today's schools.*

If you give an A effort in school, you succeed every time. But in real life, If you give an A effort in life, you're lucky to succeed on the 30th try. Bill Gates lost his first business, Steve Jobs was once fired from the same company Apple which he founded, Albert Einstein had to repeat a research for more than ten thousand times before final breakthrough, and Michael Jordan missed more shots than anyone in history. School trains us to have the mindset that a given amount of effort will always bring a measurable, predictable, and successful result. The real world doesn't work like that. Things don't work that way. Never!

Most students, when they enter the real world and are turned down for a job in favor of the janitor's son, they might take it personally. When they have to submit too many applications and interviews they get weary and disturbed. Why? They aren't mentally prepared for failures and temporary setbacks. Perhaps the interviewer didn't like them because of an unfair, deep-rooted bias. Other times it's another thing entirely. But really, they can't just wrap their heads around having to put in a measured amount of work, compile an impressive resume, say all of the right things in the interview, and yet be turned down. It's a terrible shock. But in real life, an entrepreneur knows that he can hire the best hands, invest the right amount of money, and leverage on necessarily platforms and technologies, and yet produce a result nowhere near a tenth of what he anticipated or even turn totally dismal. School never teaches that whatever the case, an A effort does not always get an A outcome on the first try. I love to close with this powerful quote below which captures it all:

The Largest Scam in History?
Go to school.
Make good grades.
Get a college degree.
Guaranteed success?
Not quite.

"Attending college has become the most socially demanded path. You don't need a four-year college degree if you have burning ambition or a great plan"

- Alan Gerry

Getting a college degree has become a goal in the chase to achieve happiness and successful person in today's America. Millions upon millions of dreams will be crushed by the propaganda being spewed by high school counselors, university marketing departments, and the federal government.

In today's world, *"college"* is more or less synonymous to *"success."* We are told from a young age that if we just attend college and graduate, we will be essentially guaranteed a career and consequent financial security for the remainder of our lives. In a sense, college is viewed as proof that you have achieved the American dream, and the rest of your life is destined for prosperity.

Your whole life, parents, teachers, coaches, have maintained that you will not be successful without a college degree, that you will amount to nothing without good grades and your head in the books.

The only problem with the *'college = success'* equation is that an academic education is not the answer for everyone. It might have been in the 1990s, even in the early 2000s, but these days, with the dire state of education, the prohibitive cost of tuition and the current high unemployment rates, there is a serious call for our youth to look at alternatives to mainstream tertiary education and be creative with their life outcomes.

Today, the value of having a degree is decreasing. But is it something everyone needs to have?

Yes, if you are an aspiring doctor, lawyer or architect.

But not all jobs require you to show a piece of paper that you are competent in your skills. Not all opportunities require you flaunt your college affiliations and history. The numbers show that nearly 50% of students who start a bachelor's degree never finish. And the average student loan debt for students in America alone is $30,000.

Don't you think the *go to school, get a good grade, and become financial free for life* rhetoric is the largest scam in history?

There are uncountable amounts of successful people and entrepreneurs who don't have university or college degrees today and thousands more joins the league every year—the likes of Oprah Winfrey, Mark Zuckerberg, Steve Jobs, Bill Gates, Steven

Spielberg, among others. These people have done remarkable things with their lives, started extraordinary businesses, inspired millions of people all over the world, and mentored even more remarkable people and enterprises. They have challenged the status quo and mainstream path, created their own stories, and achieved their wildest dreams. They have made enough and gave enough away to philanthropy, brought smiles to the many, and changed the narrative of human history. Anybody can join their ranks, but at least you'll start off from somewhere, and that is why you have this book. I'm sure herein you will find all the necessary encouragement, stories, motivation, inspiration, and guidance to get you started with maximizing whatever you have now to create the kind of life you have always imagined for yourself.

There are stuff about college that reveal lots of wrongs and sets the record straight:

The Case With Debt

According to research, more than 50% of American students have $30,000 of debt when they graduate. Over 44.2 percent are saddled with student loan debt. According to research from Student Loan Hero, the delinquency rate is more than 11.2% and the average monthly student loan payment for borrowers 20 to 30 years old is around $351. Yet, college degrees are becoming more expensive each year meaning that this debt issue isn't going to get any better soon.

To pay the price of a certificate, you must effectively mortgage your life and the return on investment for these college degrees is often much below the burden of debt acquired. Debt isn't good for anybody and starting your life with it probably leaves your dream dead until you are 40. I think the early years of adulthood were intended for people to build their lives, not dig themselves out of a hole. Young adults in their 20's and 30's are no more buying homes according to recent studies. They are waiting until their debt-to-income ratio is healthier. A meaningful portion of their lives only starts at their early 40.

What a life!

Think about what would happen if you didn't have that worry about a loan payment. You could invest that the same few hundred to thousand dollars into your own business or self-learning to create the kind of career and income stream you're looking for. You could use that to invest in your life and push your way ahead of the poverty cycle. Student debt can crush your dream. While you'll still be figuring out how to improve your income-to-debt ratio, your age mates are thousand dollars up in financial worth. The burden of debt really isn't good for anybody not to talk of student loan debt which is the only debt that can't be removed even if you go bankrupt. Having it in early 20's has been shown to push off marriage and children, increases stress and anxiety, and trigger a deep resentment towards life. This is what college nowadays is all about. No wonder former US president Barack Obama hinted that: *'folks can make a lot more by learning a trade than they might with an art history degree.'*

Education Is Relatively Inexpensive

Seen the movie Good Will Hunting, where Matt Damon's character, Will Hunting said this: *"You wasted $ 150,000 on an education you could have got for a buck fifty in late charges at the public library?"*

He was dam right! Information itself is inexpensive and easily accessible. There are online sources that offer university classes for free and the public library is there across nearly every city, big and small. You can choose to carry books with you anywhere in the world. You can download revolutionary, empowering audio programs for free and listen to it on your daily commute and even when doing your chores. You can read as many biographies as you want and study the lives of successful people. Success leaves clues. And remember, the idea is to be educated, not to be schooled.

No Guarantees

Many people attend college with the mentality that they are going to find a dream job, make an awful lot of money and their lives are going to be better thereafter once they graduate. A college degree won't guarantee you a high-paying job. It won't even make you a skilled leader with a shot at the corner office. As much as we are in the digital era, we are also in the creativity and skills era. What guarantees a high-paying job is when you have a very marketable skill that is in high demand. If you have such a skill and can bring value to lots of people and business, something like social media skills, selling skills, marketing skills, copywriting, ghostwriting, among others, you can easily make 300k a year, even beyond. Don't fall for the implied guarantee that a college degree is your ticket to lasting success. These are skills which cannot be acquired in the classroom. How I wish people put the same amount of time and energy they'd spend completing a college degree into trying out internships, exploring options for apprenticeships, maximize online education in order to learn and acquire marketable, high-paying skills, they will, for sure, do far better.

Finding Purpose Isn't Sure

This sounds like a bogus statement, but it's actually the truth. College students are fund of using the phrase *"finding yourself"*. Most young people haven't discovered what they want to do with their lives as at the time of choosing college, so the belief is that a 4-year degree buys them the time to make that decision.

Colleges takes advantages of that and brand themselves as the place young people can find themselves only for some of them to graduate 3 years later with an extra $80,000 in debt and the same inability to make it in the workforce.

But that isn't always true. *A college campus is a protected world. It's not a real world.*

A man doesn't find himself by being caged. A man finds himself by doing things, by developing his skills, *by finding his gifts*, by testing his strength, by exploring his ideas and projects in the real world, and by failing and failing and picking up again until he gets it right. That is how it works in the real world. That is how to break even and become successful. A man only finds his true self by putting himself into challenging situations. That is the easiest way to find out what you are worth.

You Could Be Left Far Behind

Imagine putting in a lot of time and money into something that may not be useful again when the time comes, and you really need it. What a massive disappointment that would be? That is how it is with college. You're putting a lot of time and money into a degree that may or may not be obsolete by the time you're ready to use it. By the time you are done, your degree could be useless already.

Even if the degree seems useful, that still isn't a pointer that you are ready for the mainstream job market. Technology and business processes and trends age quickly and changes so fast that it might be hard to keep up with changing trends when you're stuck behind your textbooks for four years.

Reflections

- Have you heard about the Gillian Lynne story before? What do you think she represents to our world today, and what does her story says about education in America?
- Imagine yourself in the role of the doctor, what would you have done? If you were the mother, what would you have honestly done?
- How do you think Gillian would have been treated in today's traditional school system?
- Do you believe that truly some children are not cut out for college?
- What, in your opinion, do you think is really wrong with our educational school system today?
- Do you think the school system as it is today can ever produce the creative minds we need in our world to provide solutions to the world's avalanche of problems?
- Do you believe the school system kills creativity? If yes, can you back it up with a personal view, opinion, or experience?
- Go to school, get good grades, get a job, etc. What do you make of that popular sentence at a personal level?
- Do you think school trains people to succeed or fail in the real world?

- Do you have a college degree? If yes, was it the most crucial decider of where you stand today financially? How can you describe the role and influence of college degree in your financial story as it stands right now?
- What do stories of great entrepreneurs like Gates, Jobs, Zuckerberg, among others quitting colleges tell you about our school system?

CHAPTER 4

You and Your Mind

If you will go on this ride with me, we've got to start with some mind de-cluttering. I strongly believe that many people's lives are in a mess today because they are looking for one magic formula that will solve all their problems at once. They read from epic stories to great biographies, attend seminars from Ohio to Sao Paulo, and are on the email list of their favorite success guru. They are on the lookout for the next big thing: the epic audio program, the phenomenal meet up, the once-a-lifetime seminar, among others, yet they never take care of the most important, basic thing which is the ability to believe that they have the ability to transform their own lives.

They have never really gotten out of the *"I can't mindset"*.

Are you where you want to be in life generally or in your career? I believe the answer is no. How do I know that? Because if you are you won't be reading this book. You see, every single thing that goes wrong in your life is because of a blame placed everywhere but with your own choices and decisions.

Do you get that at all?

What I mean is that whether you want to admit it or not, you are the one directly responsible for all the outcomes of your life. You are the one, not situations, not circumstances, not 9/11, not your country's economy, not inflation, not Al Qaeda, but you! Where you currently are in life is as a result of your mindset. That is where everything starts. You have to accept complete responsibility for your life and where you currently are on your journey. When you accept complete responsibility for your life, you begin to easily exercise the power to transform it. Instantly, you win back to your side all the energy you have ceded to situations and circumstances. You start being in charge of your life. You give no more excuses. You start to do all that it takes to change the direction of your life and create the life of your dreams. Making excuses out of everything becomes a thing of the past. It's all about your mind.

The difference between the rich and the poor is basically the mind. To change the direction and the quality of your life, you have to change your mindset, get your head right and in the game. You start from building up an unshakable possibility mindset. You set up an *"I can do it fire"* around you. When the fire of possibility is up, amazing things begin to happen in your mind. You stop the negatives. You start each day with belief. You start to part ways and cut off from toxic and goalless people in your life. You start to see clearly that you don't have to be shackled by the experience your parents went through. You don't have to suffer as they suffered.

You can't make money without the right mindset, and even if you made lots of it somehow without the right mindset, you'll still lose everything. That is the reason virtually all lotto winners go back broke and poor. It all starts from the mind. And that is where we should start the journey from. When the mind is fixed, everything else always falls in place.

Impossibility Is a Myth

Nothing is impossible.

This is the first thing I'll like you to know as we start on this journey. See, impossibility is a myth. It is an illusion. It is nothing but a construct in the mind of men. Can you do me a favor please? Grab your dictionary and strike the word *"impossible"* out. If you must be successful and achieve all your dreams in life and make lots of money in any endeavor you choose, then that word is never meant for you. It doesn't belong in your lexicon. You've got to strike out that poison from your mind.

We have all been there before. It's alright. It's easy to give up. It's easy to throw in the towel. It's not out of place to think that your dreams are impossible and unachievable. It is not strange if the words *"I can't"* and *"It's impossible"* has become your final bus stop and has shaped every of your words, actions, dreams, aspirations, and beliefs. It's like for whatever you can do or bring, the phrase seems the most powerful.

Yes, you might have the economy very tough on you, almost getting you over the edge. Yes, you might have customers demanding more than ever from you and your company. Yes, your ex has rejected advances of reconciliation for the past nine months, leaving you to reel hopelessly in the guilt of having to let her go in the first place. Yes, the weight of debt on you is like a milestone tied around your neck. Yes, all your efforts to start a new business and create a good life for you and your family have been unfruitful. Yes, you felt lost, deserted, betrayed, and felt like you cannot trust anyone except yourself again. I understand you. Many have been there before.

But I'm not sympathizing with you.

Why? Because instead of focusing on all that is happening on the outside which practically sells you the idea of *"impossibility"*, you should look inward and believe in yourself that you can do anything in life that you want to do. You can make anything happen. You can believe, birth, and become whatever you set your mind upon. You can create your universe. You can change your situation. You can literally print your cash in this digital economy *if you can follow the due process*. It's more than possible.

Nothing else teaches you impossibility as your mind. The only impossibility exists within your mind. It's your mind that set things as impossible or possible. It is your mind that says you won't do this or that. But I think you have more than enough reasons to think possibility. Isn't it?

For a moment, forget all the grass-to-great narratives you read in books and biographies, in prints, and see in late night TVs. Look around you and you'll see there are leagues of ordinary people around you whose life successes have proven that the word *"Impossible"* is nonexistent for anyone that wants winning in life bad enough.

The human mind understands no impossibilities except the one you feed it with. Ask yourself, how did we end up flying in the air from Khartoum to Seoul? How did we end up with using the sun's energy in our homes as solar power? How did we end up communicating with a device from a distance as far as Ouagadougou to Saint Petersburg? How did the America flag come to be on the moon? How did surrogacy come to be? Where on earth did Harry Porter and Lord of the Rings come from? Consider how Google, Facebook, Apple, and Starbucks came into existence?

All these first existed in the minds of some people. It's the same way achieving your dreams and living your purpose exists in your mind right now. Impossible is a word you should hate more than whatever you hate most in reality.

The amazing thing about the mind is that when you believe something is possible, it will find means to make it happen. It will unleash your creativity and genius and you'll feel in a state of empowerment. In the early 1950s, many people believed that it was impossible for humans to run a mile in under four minutes. Runners had been trying to break the four-minute barrier since the late 1800s to no avail. The world's top coaches and most gifted athletes had been trying for years. They were dedicated, and they'd tried all sorts of training plans, but the milestone was believed to be out of reach. It was believed that the human body just couldn't go that fast.

Then it finally happened—the seemingly impossible. Roger Bannister, in 1954, ran the mile in 3 minutes 59.4 seconds. A month and a half later, John Landy ran even faster. Three more runners broke the four minutes barrier a year later. Today, high school runners break the barrier routinely.

You see that impossibility is a myth?

You see, this thing about having a possibility mentality is a very serious matter and the foundation of any success you want to achieve in life. Think of Oprah Winfrey. As a kid, she wore potato sacks because clothing did not always fit into the budget of her poverty-stricken family. She suffered a tumultuous childhood. She shuffled between family members, spending her first few years on her grandmother's farm in rural Mississippi while her unwed teenage mom looked for work. Later, at 6 years old, she joined her mother in a Milwaukee boarding house, where she would not only grow up around extreme poverty, but also endured years of sexual and physical abuse. She was raped by her 19year old cousin and that was the beginning of several episodes of sexual and emotional assaults on the young girl. At age 14, Winfrey went to live with her dad in Nashville, Tennessee. Despite insecurity and deep emotional issues, she carried from traumas, she thrived academically in East Nashville High School where she became an honor roll student and was voted the most popular girl in her class. She discovered her passion for media and dream of becoming the greatest woman media mogul. She joined the speech team and worked for a local black radio station after school. By her senior year she had secured a full scholarship to Tennessee State University.

At 19, she dropped out of college to pursue a career in media and before age 20 she already became the first black female news anchor in Nashville. At Baltimore, in a co-anchor position, she was sexually harassed and humiliated and eventually fired seven and half months after joining. She didn't stay down. She believed in her dreams and maintained her fire to reach for the stars. She landed a gig hosting the then-stagnant morning talk show *"AM Chicago"* and within a few months turned from the lowest-rated talk show in Chicago to the highest-rated one. She renamed it the Oprah Winfrey Show three years later. She found Harpo productions and negotiated the ownership of the show in 1986 which brought her about $300 million a year as at 1986. Her company also produced award-winning spinoff shows like *"Dr. Phil"* and *"Rachael Ray."* She became a media mogul and queen of Daytime TV, a filmmaker, television series producer, and an academy award nominee for best supporting actress in the 1985 drama *"The Color Purple."* She launched her own magazine, *The Oprah Magazine*, started a radio channel, *Oprah Radio*, and partnered with Discovery Communications to launch a cable channel, the *Oprah Winfrey Network*. Today, the girl who wore potato-sack overalls now dons Prada and Jimmy Choo, flies in her own $42 million, custom-designed Global Express XRS jet, has all manner of estate properties, farmhouses, vacation homes, and a ski villa, etc. all over the world, and even has a street named after her and was, at a time, the richest black woman in the world.

Judging by her traumatic childhood, all these seemed impossible. But she believed!

Form Your Own Beliefs

I strongly believe that the most reason why the average man has a hard time believing is because they've never done it. What I mean is that they never really formed their own beliefs.

Think about it.

Just take a moment and trace back all your beliefs on religion, politics, money, people, society, and the world in general? You'll figure out in the eventuality that the root of the majority of your beliefs sourced from friends, parents, colleagues, media, Hollywood, etc. and not you. You were fed stuffs like:

"Go to school, get good grades, graduate, get a great job, and become successful."
"Don't talk to strangers, they are evil."
"Money is the root of all evil." (The bible actually wrote that the love of money is the root of all evil, not money itself.) "It's difficult to start a business. Most fail."
"Everything you hear about people making money online is fake."
"You cannot depend on people, it's only God that is dependable on." "Men are cheats. They'll always cheat on you no matter how you care for them."

You have probably heard many, if not all of these from all sorts of sources: friends, parents, Hollywood, etc. You can't deny that they have somehow slipped into your subconscious, become to you ruling beliefs, controlling every step of your life and shaping every aspect of your existence. What you don't mostly admit is that those beliefs handed down to you came from their life experiences and not the actual truth.

A perfect conclusion we can deduce from this is that you have long been controlled by forces beyond you that you have allowed for so long. The majority of people have never really gone through the exercise of creating their own beliefs because they've been spoon-fed by other sources from day one.

Now it's time to be fed what the 1 percent believe.

It is time to form your own beliefs.

To believe you can do anything in life, you must have a strong foundational belief that you can. Whatever you want to do in life, whoever you want to become in destiny, you must first, and most importantly, have the *"I Can Do It"* Spirit. You have to be able to convince yourself that you can pull it off. It's never enough in life to just say, *"Oh, I believe, and it will happen."* Nothing great and spectacular in this universe came into being that way. That is another kind of way people express impossibility.

It's time to take charge of your own beliefs. And to be able to do that, you must know how to believe. You must understand the process in which some of the most powerful beliefs in human beings are created. For example, imagine people's beliefs rooted in religion and politics. They are extremely powerful. Millions of lives are taken because of indifferences as seen in various needless wars across the world. Families became divided over them. People take their own lives because of them as mostly exhibited by suicide bombers. We fought other kids over them when we were young. Clearly, you would agree that the power of people's belief in religion and politics and the effect it has on their lives is unquestioned.

If we can analyze the procedure in which these beliefs were formed and apply the same method to creating our own beliefs too, then we will be able to achieve anything we want to in life. We will be able to easily print our own money. Nothing will look impossible. So, the next question is: How do you form your beliefs?

STEP 1: You Must State a Specific Belief First

There are many people in life who do not believe in anything. You ask them,

"Do you think you can buy your dream beach house before 40?" You hear responses like, *"I don't know…maybe…. we'll see."* Let's say you are sited across me at a beach right now and I ask you, *"Can you make at least 300k a year?"* What would be your answer? Would your mind quickly drift to how you have never been able to make even 40k a year for the first 30 years of your life or you would just believe that it's high time you changed and dared to dream? You must have a specific belief you believe in. It doesn't matter if you don't believe it at first. Just take the first step and STATE it.

Let's use this example in the paragraph above: *"I will buy my dream apartment before 40."*

A specific belief has been created and the first step has been taken. That is the starting point. Something has begun.

Now let's say the current reality is that you are still managing in a rented apartment in a less-developed area and still struggling with paying some of your recurring bills. I can imagine what you are thinking: *"I can't buy such an apartment even in my dreams. Such are always expensive. I am struggling with debts. Where do I get that kind of money from? I still can't pay my bills regularly. I am 35 already and we are talking about just 5 years from now."* If that is your automatic reaction, it's very fine. It is normal to feel recoil whenever you attempt to think beyond the horizon and dream big. It is normal to hit an instant mental brick wall anytime you dare to make far more than what you're currently making. I'm not going to tell you to change your self-talk for now because I understand it's hard to do so. No need to get overwhelmed or discouraged. It's one step at a time. Now that you have stated a specific belief, what is next?

STEP 2: Hammer That Belief into Yourself Repeatedly and Continuously

Know this truth please: *Beliefs are not formed overnight.* All the powerful beliefs people hold about religion and politics did not develop in their minds overnight. It came as a result of constant hammering of information over a long period of time. Most extremist you see today have been indoctrinated right from childhood. They learned of such beliefs from all manner of sources. Whether it was their teacher at High School, friends in the baseball practice sessions, instructor at the gym, parents over dinner table, or a religious service, among others, a particular source must have repeatedly hammered it into their ears, thereby reinforcing it in their minds. Books, magazines, TV, Internet, and all manners of public demonstrations like marches and movements play their parts too.

No forces, human or circumstantial, are there to hammer any beliefs in you now. I am teaching you to how to create your *Own Belief* and *Hammer* it into *yourself* as a matter of personal responsibility.

It doesn't matter if you do not believe in the beginning. It doesn't matter if shooting your income to 400k a year seems like Mount Everest in your eyes right now. It doesn't matter even if your self-talk is negating your belief. Hammering your belief in gets you beyond that stage. If you continuously *hammer* it in, the nail will always go right into the wall of your mind. This is the reason many people fail.

It is the reason 90% of people conclude that the whole *"If you believe you can achieve it"* idea is a farce. This is a generation where the virtue of patience and perseverance has gone down the drain. We live in an instantaneous society. We want results NOW. With a click of a mouse we can access all sorts of information. A push of a button and we have music, video, news, and entertainment instantly. We are spoiled and distracted. We become easily discouraged when we don't see quick results. We have lost the notion of sticking through with something and not quitting no matter how long it takes until it is achieved. That is why we must continuously focus on hammering in our new beliefs. Let me show few tricks that definitely help in hammering in your new belief right into the core of your mind.

Write It Down

Jim Carrey was an unknown actor struggling to get by in the early 1990s. He wrote himself a check for $10 million and labeled it *"For Acting Services Rendered"* so as to stay motivated. He dated it 1994 and carried it in his wallet for daily inspiration. When 1994 came, $10 million was all for grabs as he learned that was the exact amount he would reap for his role in *Dumb and Dumber*. Today, he is one of the most in-demand American Hollywood greats.

Remember Scott Adams the famous Dilbert cartoon strip?

He wrote daily that he would become rich in the stock market. Soon, by stroke of magic, he invested in *Chrysler and Ask* which were two of the best performing stocks at the time and he made a very decent profit. He tried it again with GMAT. He wrote it down that he would hit the 94th percentile even though he had only scored at the 77th percentile when taking several tests. When the results came in he hit exactly 94th percentile. He gained so much conviction in the power of writing down beliefs that he believed he would become a famous syndicated cartoonist.

Guess what? That is what he is renowned for today globally.

Place It Everywhere You Can See It

After writing your belief on paper or printed out, paste it everywhere you can see it: mirror, door, on your refrigerator, computer, TV, front door, bathroom, just everywhere. You can make it your computer's default home screensaver and your phone's. You can put it on a reminder on your gadgets. Carry it everywhere. Have a piece of it in your wallet or purse. Let it be all that you see. Let it consume you through and through. Scott Adams placed it everywhere he could see it. Jim Carrey carried it around in his wallet. This way, you will drill the belief into yourself and from time to time, it becomes stronger than at the point of writing it down. Write yours boldly on a white paper, A2 or any that suits you.

Visualize That Your Belief Has Already Been Achieved Every Day

Let me tell you one big truth: *Your brain does not know the difference between what is visible and what isn't. It does not know the difference between what it sees with your eyes and what you imagine with your mind.* That is why you can feel good when you are sure of a credit alert coming soon even though you don't see it in your balance yet. Your brain cannot really interpret the difference. Reality lives alone in the brain.

Because of this truth, you can create your reality of already having achieved your belief by visualizing it in order to help HAMMER the belief into your brain. Rome was not built in a day.

You must take time each day to hammer your belief in. If you do it sporadically, your belief will never take root. There are no shortcuts in life, and you know that's true deep down within you. Anything worthy of significant value wasn't created instantaneously. That is where visualization comes in. It's another powerful exercise you can do.

Scott Adams and Jim Carry didn't just write and carried their belief everywhere, they visualized consistently living in the reality of that belief. As a young athlete, Arnold Schwarzenegger used the power of visualization to reach his bodybuilding goals. He had the idea of a body like Reg Park fixed in his mind. He only had to grow enough to become it. The more he focused on this image and worked and grew, the more he saw it was real and possible for him to be like Park. When he moved into acting and politics, he used the same techniques. *"What you do is create a vision of who you want to be—and then live that picture as if it were already true."*

For Oprah Winfrey to get to the summit today, she stayed committed to this same technique. As a child watching her grandmother toil away, Winfrey says she'd tell herself over and over again: *"My life won't be like this. My life won't be like this, it will be better."*

Lindsey Vonn, one of the most successful female skiers in history and Olympic gold medalist used the same technique to have a competitive edge. According to her, she always visualizes the runs before she does it actually. By the time she gets started, she'd run the race already 100 times in her head, picturing how she'll take the turns. She also practiced how to physically stimulate the path by literally shifting her weight back and forth as though she were on skis as well as mastering the specific breathing patterns she'll use during the race.

> *"Create the highest, grandest vision possible for your life, because you become what you believe."*
>
> **- Oprah Winfrey**
> *(Talk-show host and media mogul)*

In the same vein as Oprah, Lindsey, Adam, and Carry, you have to visualize having achieved your dreams already. Imagine all that changed in your life after you have achieved your dreams, and how happy and fired up you'll be to do even more. Use those images to drive your mind into believing you have reached the goal.

STEP 3: Be Determined to Associate With Those Who Share Your Beliefs

Look at anyone you know with a strong religious or political belief; you'll find out that they have a continuous association with those who shared the same views and sentiments. It is such affiliations that help to solidify their respective beliefs. Naturally, people do not hang around those who do not share their beliefs. Doing so means they'll be open to contrary beliefs which could weaken their conviction. You don't see Jews and Muslim sharing any kind of affiliation and you'll hardly see an association between hardcore conservatives and liberals.

The rich get richer and the poor poorer, they say. It's all down to association. People who share same belief naturally gravitate towards one another. It is an indisputable fact of life. Naturally, you'll find out that the more you HAMMER your beliefs in, the more it sinks in, the more you'll become uncomfortable with your current association if it's contradictory to what you intend to bring into your life by virtue of your stated beliefs. You'll start to gravitate towards those who share the same beliefs.

It's a great sign that you are moving in the right, positive direction the moment you notice this. It shows your beliefs are taking over you. And that is exactly what you want. Naturally, you will find yourself looking for those who share the same belief for advice, mentorship, or support. Your book titles will begin to change. Your favorite talk show may begin to suck and you'll have to start watching another in the line of your beliefs. Lots of things will start to change.

STEP 4: You Must Confirm Your Belief in Your Environment

If you can manage to consistently hammer your belief in yourself and surround yourself with those who shared same belief, you will soon start to see a confirmation of your belief in your environment.

For anything you believe in and want to be, there is someone, who somehow, is already living the reality in your environment. The greatest evidence that something can be done is if another person has done it. So, the question is how many people in life who came from a background of extreme poverty became successful in life and made a whole lot of money? I'm sure you can, at least, mention 10 to 20 at a go. If you dig enough, there are thousands, if not millions of them all over the world who have created a very successful career for themselves and living the lives of their dreams.

As you begin to move in the direction of your belief you'll begin to see them everywhere. You'll see them on TV, read about them in the news, meet them at a function, or even connect with them in social media groups like Facebook, WhatsApp, or Telegram. Collect the inspirational stories of these people. That is one of the reasons why reading biographies of people who have become successful in the path you have chosen is still one of the best reading choices you can ever make in your life. Refer to those and through the eyes of their successes and achievements, confirm and reinforce your belief whenever it seems shaky or fading.

STEP 5: Take Massive Action

After you have stated your belief, hammered it into yourself repetitively, frequently affiliated with those who share the same belief, and confirming it in your environment, the next thing is to take massive action. This step won't be any harder because you have laid the foundation of belief already. The more hammered in your beliefs are, the higher the degree of the actions you'll take.

This is where most people get it wrong. They put the cart before the horse. They try to take action first without really laying the foundation of a strong belief that they can. Today you say you have the belief that you can buy your dream beach house before 40 and tomorrow you have started pricing ranges of available options in Hawaii and Arizona. That is stupid and futile. You are still struggling with debt and your business is just really taking off as it has been surviving on loans from here and there as life support. Then what happens? After learning that the one you'll love cost somewhere between 300k to 1 million dollars then your brain shuts down immediately. You realized you have gone too far and that's not your level.

You know exactly what I'm talking about! You have only shot yourself in the foot.

You should have taken it bit by bit and laid a strong belief foundation and the more you hammer it in the more you'll know you can because belief shapes reality. If you've done a good job of drilling the belief into yourself, you will find it easy to take action towards it.

STEP 6: Acknowledge Progress Made

You've stated a specific belief and hammered it to yourself continuously. You have rolled into associations and formed alliances with those who share the same beliefs. You have reinforced your belief by even confirming it in your environment by meeting some investment experts in person for discussions or taken up as a mentor an Internet marketing guru who does more than 10 million dollars in sales annually. You have also taken action to fulfill your belief by setting some clear money goals. Let's say after meeting a mentor who shares same belief as yours, you were told that you have to learn basic selling skills on the Internet. After the first two weeks, you were able to create a sales page for a product. Celebrate that! You are on your way to your dreams. If you can do for that first month, then you can take the next, and the next, and another step, until you reach your goals.

At this point, your belief will start to grow exponentially. Acknowledging your own progress solidifies your belief. The moment you notice such progresses, document it. Don't just trust it to your memory.

When you have it written down, you can always refer to it to strengthen your belief at any point in time.

STEP 7: Repeat, Repeat, and Repeat

This process must be repeated severally, especially from steps 2-6. Beliefs to do the impossible do not form overnight. It takes time, discipline, and perseverance which is the reason most people shy away from it. They'll rather take the easiest path which is to give up. Now you know that if you believe you can do anything, you can actually do it. Now you know the exact process how to believe and in turn, achieve.

You Need To Really Mean It

You will get nothing in life if you don't really mean it.

If there is something I wanted you to learn from the examples I've shared in this book, it is that that those people who became successful did so because they never gave up. For every disappointment, they pushed harder, and for every failed strategy, they became more creative. Whether they dropped out to launch their own ideas straightaway or work in an industry before creating their own brands, one common denominator is that they had a clear focus and a realistic goal in mind. They really meant it, were intentional about it, and would never take no for an answer until they have seen the reality of their mental pictures.

You cannot take anything in life at face value and not fail at it. If you take on an unrealistic goal, you are doomed to fail from the start. Imagine saying you want to lose 30 pounds in 30 days in the gym? Imagine desiring to be the world greatest karate master within the space of six months when you have a strong aversion for even the mildest of exercises? Imagine you want to become the first man to plant American flag on the sun? Or how about saying you want to make a 100m dollars within 3 months selling on the Internet when you have never made a dollar over the years? All these are unrealistic goals and no matter how much you claim you believe in them you won't achieve anything. This is an example of when the phrase *success comes to those who believe* is applied wrongly.

Let us consider a common realistic goal like desiring to hit 300k over a year in sales from your newly launched e-commerce store. What did you do? You dedicated your time to read more about scaling up your store, met marketing experts, watched many online videos on e-commerce, got on the email list and subscribed to YouTube channels of top guys in the industry, paid for webinars, etc. Let's say in the end you were only able to make 80k after a year and your ads budget was already red. Then you give up. Things weren't going according to your plan and you just quitted.

The truth is this: *You are the one that stopped yourself.*

That's not setting your mind to something. If you really, truly set your mind to something, there is no way of someone or something stopping you. You will try again, and again, and again. You may have to re-strategize or even overhaul your marketing efforts. You might have to recruit some virtual assistance. You might have to connect to better mentors who are killing it in e-commerce, in person. If you really mean it, you would cross the world and take on anything in your path to acquire what you desire. That's what great people do, from world-class entrepreneurs and athletes, to fictional characters like Spiderman, Dr. Strange, and The Black Panther.

See, the world is filled with people who give up and then complain about it.

Consider the last example and let's say that you are the guy with the e-commerce store. Did you achieve your goal? No? Then get back up and try again. If you don't get to meet your dream target, it's an opportunity to learn how to do it better. If you give up, that's on you. Remember that in real life what qualifies you for the 'A's most time is the many 'F's that has gone into your story. Anybody who is successful in any way has experienced failures—lots of them—and if they had given up after the first, second, or 200th, they wouldn't have become as successful at all. Most of the great things that has come to be as part of our existence today, in groundbreaking scientific discoveries, great companies, among others, won't be there if those who conceived them never tried again and again after initial failures with them.

Really, it is hard to take in an indefinite amount of failure. It's painful to have it all mapped out only to see it crumble before your eyes when you least expected. Of a truth, people often decide for the easier option which is to simply give up and quit. Really I know it is really hard to take in. Everyone isn't an Albert Einstein or Henry Ford. While some feed on these failures and disappointments and use it as energy to propel them further, most people simply say *"fuck it"*, find a job they hate, kick back in front of the TV after work, stopped visiting the library, stopped attending seminars, and never aspire to do much. But the truth remains that, if you must break away from the poverty cycle and achieve your dreams in life, you'll have to give it all it takes irrespective of the initial setbacks or disappointment you encounter.

Reflections

- Honestly, who and what have you always blamed all these years for your circumstances? After reading this chapter, who do you now blame?
- How does it feel to accept all the blame for your circumstances and accept it's up to you to fix your life? Empowering or burdening?
- Do you believe the journey to wealth starts from your mind? Explain.
- How about forming your own beliefs? Did you follow the procedure as laid out in the chapter? If yes, what were the old beliefs you omitted about money and life? What are the new ones you have taken up?

CHAPTER 5 Take the Responsibility

- Yes, the government isn't coming for you.
- And yes, you are right if you think the system rips you off.
- You also know better how going to college is not a ticket out of poverty.

Now you know that the chance of you doing better compared to your parents and grandparents who never really enjoyed financial freedom won't lead you to the kind of life you seek. To become different and travel along a new path that leads to wealth and purpose, you know you've got to master what the 1 percent know and do. You know you have to follow the process.

But how do you even start and bring all these together? Is there really a way out?

Yes, there is. To break even in America today even if you currently wallow somewhere at the bottom of the chain, and change the narrative of your life for good, you'll have to follow the process.

The starting point of everything is when you come to that point where you take the scruff of your life by the neck and take absolute responsibility for your life.

That is the first door you'll have to pull through to break any cycle of poverty.

Whatever is it that success means to you, there are thousands of people in history who have already achieved that which you want in life, right?

That is very interesting because it means that it can be done by you also if you can follow the "clues" they left behind.

I loved what H. L. Hunt, who was once the richest man in the world, said when he was asked what the secrets of his success were. He replied:

"There are only three requirements for success. First, decide exactly what it is you want in life. Second, determine the price that you are going to have to pay to get the things you want. And third, and this is most important, resolve to pay the price." Isn't that very straightforward?

You see, everyone wants to be successful. Almost everyone has some money goals written somewhere in the walls of their minds. Millions of people want to break away from the poverty trap. They want to move from *"poor and middle class"* to the *"1 percent of the world"*. But what I'm 100 percent sure of is that everyone is not willing *to pay the price*. Most people are not willing to pay the price. Occasionally, they may be willing to pay *part* of the price, but they are not willing to pay the *whole* price. They aren't ready for whatever shift they've got to put in and for as long as it takes, until they have achieved the results they desire. They don't want it bad enough.

Somehow I believe that for you personally, you have an idea or a measure of what success means to you. When you are not working *"deliberately, consciously, and continuously to do, be, and have those things that constitute that success for you, you default to the path of least resistance, or to the expediency path—neither of which lead to success"*.

Instead, they will lead to cutting corners and getting things done just to get them out of the way, but not to put in the work to do them right necessarily.

What is now the price of success, perhaps you are asking?

It's simple.

Just look around you and there it is. You can always tell how much of the price of success you have paid by looking at your current lifestyle and your bank account.

And I'm sure that reflects that you haven't really stretched yourself to achieve the life of your dreams and make the kind of money you feel you deserve consistently.

There are many prices to be paid if you must reach your money goal, among other goals in life. One of it is learning from the experts and those whose past achievements are the dreams you currently nurse and the vision you're looking forward to. Another price is to learn all you can about what it takes and after finding out, do them continuously, every day. Once you begin, you never stop until your life and career are over and you have achieved all the success you desire. Often times, the price is hard and tough, but when you accept them and do them consistently, they become to you habits, and at that point, you can get anything you want because the price has become your very nature.

Success is very predictable. Why? Because it leaves clues and the clues are often the same even though the stories are from diverse backgrounds. Your current set of thoughts, character, attitudes, choices, values, ethics, among others, got you to where you are today financially and if you continue just like that, you and I can easily predict your next 1, 3, 7, 10 years. Likewise, if you want to change the direction of your life, break out of the cycle of poverty, and achieve your target financial goal within the next 1 to 3 years, you'll have to adopt new set of values, beliefs, and attitudes, among others, that served great people who have gone ahead of you very well. So, in the real sense, all it really takes you to achieve your goal is to model the principles that worked for those that have gone ahead of you and have achieved not just same, but bigger goals than you currently desire.

When you model them passionately and adopt what works, they become a part of you. By then, you have successfully built successful and wealthy habits.

Take 100 Percent Responsibility for Your Life

"You must take personal responsibility. You cannot change the circumstances, the seasons, or the wind, but you can change yourself."

- Jim Rohn

America's foremost business philosopher

I love the conversation in Jack Canfield's *"How to Get from Where You Are to Where You Want to be."* It was between Jack himself and America's premier success guru W. Clement Stone who was the publisher of Success magazine, author of *"The Success System That*

Never Fails," and coauthor with Napoleon Hill on *"Success through a Positive Mental Attitude."*

In the book, Jack was just completing his first week of orientation and Mister Stone started his interview.

He asked, "John, do you take 100 percent responsibility for your life?"

John responded with "I think so."

Mister Stones pressed him further. "This is a yes or no question, young man you either do or you don't."

"Well, I guess I'm not sure," Jack admitted.

Then Mister Stone hit the bull's eye! "Have you ever blamed anyone for any circumstances in your life? Have you ever complained about anything?" "Uh…yeah…. I guess I have." *(You see the word "guess." That's how we are naturally wired. We always want to put the responsibility on another person.)*

"Don't guess. Think."

"Yes, I have."

"Okay, then. That means you don't take 100 percent responsibility for your life."

He continued: "Taking 100 percent responsibility means you acknowledge you create everything that happens to you. It means you understand you are the cause of all your experiences. If you want to be really successful, and I know you do, then you will have to give up blaming and complaining and take total responsibility for your life—that means all the results, both your successes and your failures. That is the prerequisite for creating a successful life.

It is only by acknowledging that you have created everything up until now that you can take charge of creating the future you want."

"You see, Jack, if you realize that you have created your current conditions, then you can un-create them and recreate them at will. Do you understand that?"

"Yes, sir, I do."

"Are you willing to take 100 percent responsibility for your life?"

"Yes, sir, I am!"

Isn't it great reading the exact words of the legendary Clement Stone himself as he said it to a young man on the fundamental step to take for anybody that desires great success and willing to pay the prize for it? And of course, we all know Jack Canfield today. He is the man that co-created *"Chicken Soup for the Soul",* the record-breaking bestseller which New York Times regard as the publishing phenomenon of the 21st century. Quitting, giving up, failing, judging—all begins with a grave excuse. You must learn how not to turn a circumstance in your life to an alibi. George Washington carver captured it well when he said,

"99 percent of all failures come from people who have a habit of making excuses." Excuses are for people who don't want it bad enough.

If you really crave to be successful, you have to take 100 percent responsibility for everything that you have experienced in your life and the ones you want to start experiencing.

I understand that we are basically wired to blame everything outside and beyond us as the reason for our condition, but that's got to change.

You have to take absolute responsibility for your life.

And listen, this is the biggest and greatest price you have to pay. When you tell yourself the truth about yourself, real changes you have to make begins.

Tell yourself that you are the reason why you are not making the money you are supposed to be making. Tell yourself you are the reason why you have not started your online marketing business. Tell yourself you are the reason why you have not started learning copywriting on Udemy. Tell yourself you are why you are where you are today. But also tell yourself that you are the only person responsible to change all of these into positive situations, and that it all depends on you.

You are the center of the universe if you would believe it. Everything revolves around you. Circumstances move when you move. Things shape up when you take a stand. When you decide to be responsible for not just the circumstances, but the outcomes you want to start seeing now from your life, the journey is half-done.

You are the reason why you have never been able to make up to XXX amount a year before in your job or business, and you are also the one responsible to make it happen. Knowing and accepting that reality is the first and most important price you've got to pay for your success.

Be responsible. You are the one getting the car keys and driving out of the mental rut that has kept you in absolute poverty.

Take complete responsibility for your life.

Reflections

- Are you willing to pay the price to get to where you should be in life?
- Success and failure are both predictable. Please explain the way you understand it.
- What is your high point from the conversation between W. Clement Stones and Jack Canfield as documented in the chapter?

CHAPTER 6

Invest In Yourself

"You are essentially who you create yourself to be and all that occurs in your life is the result of your own making."

-Stephen Richards

A CEO of a company earns millions for working 8 hours and an intern in the same company manages to grab a few dollars for working the same period of time or even more. WHY?

The reason is because you get paid for value you bring to a company or the world and not for the time you put into that particular area. The intern probably works tirelessly all day, using all his physical strength, energy and effort but still can't manage to fulfill basic necessities of life. And there is the CEO who flies in helicopters and private jets and enjoys all manner of perks that extends to his family, yet he works for far less hours.

Why is this so? Why is the all the hard work and effort not paying off? You see, the value we give is directly tied to the level of investment we have made on ourselves and that is probably the biggest difference between the CEO and the intern.

Income rarely exceeds personal development.

Sometimes income takes a lucky jump, but unless you learn to handle the responsibilities that come with it, it will usually shrink back to the amount you can handle. We all have this thing inside us that works like a financial thermostat. You know thermostats right? When we suddenly earn big money or a windfall that maybe we have never earned before, we begin to self-sabotage. How? We become very uncomfortable with it. We, before then, had always thought all we needed was so much money but when it comes, it actually brings a measure of discomfort. To ease ourselves and get back to our comfort zone which is a measure of what we can handle, we begin to spend lavishly, start buying what we don't need, borrow friends that we know might not return it back, and make all the wrong choices with investment scams. Until we are left with the amount we are comfortable with, the amount we have been used to and always handled, we feel no peace. The thermostats always regulate us back to our true level of financial mindset. And this happens whenever our income exceeds our personal development.

Let me take you a bit into the world of lottery. According to a study done by wolf street, nearly one-third of U.S. lottery winners declare bankruptcy, often within just a few years of their big win.

William Post III won $16.2 million in a 1988 Pennsylvania lottery. Post experienced crime, bankruptcy and poor spending decisions, such as the purchase of a restaurant and an airplane got him worse than before he won the windfall. In the early 1990s, he filed for bankruptcy and was already more than $500,000 in debt.

Evelyn Marie Adams won the New Jersey lottery twice in 1985 and 1986 ($5.4 million). In a New York Post in 2012, she admitted to being broke after excessive gambling that took away majority of the money in Atlantic City.

Andrew Whittaker was already worth $17 million when he received a lump sum payout of over $170 million won in lottery. He donated to charities and foundations. He divorced, lost his granddaughter, and then began drinking heavily.

Janite Lee won $18 million. After donating loads of money to the Democratic National Committee, as well individual political candidates and Washington University and its law school, Lee filed for bankruptcy with only $700 left to her name. She had reportedly lost roughly $350,000 gambling.

Denise Rossi won a lottery of $1.3 million. After that, her first action was to divorce her husband, who had no knowledge of the win. In 1999, the ex-husband sued and the judge declared that Rossi had violated state asset-disclosure laws. As a result, the ex-husband received all of the winnings.

Couples Alex and Rhoda Toth accepted payments of $666,666 over a 20-year span in 1990 but filed for bankruptcy in 2006 after living lavish lifestyles in Vegas and enduring a sleuth of legal expenses resulting from family drama. The couple was later charged with tax evasion. Rhoda was sentenced to two years in prison and was fined $1.1 million. Less than 2 years after Billie

Bob Harrell Jr. won $31 million, he had taken his own life. While alive, he paid bills and bought new cars and homes for his family before purchasing roughly 500 turkeys for the poor.

When you examine these people's lives critically, what do you see? You'll see a trend of self-sabotage with all of them which are reckless actions that can only guarantee them one thing which is send them back to how they've been before the windfall came, or even much worse. It ranged from divorce, family drama, and binge and lavish spending decisions, unreasonable money commitment to friends, family, strangers, or even the clear at the liquor store, among many others.

See, the reason these people lost all they had was because they were never ready for the money that came their way. They were never prepared for it. The man and woman that they were had not built up the strength of responsibility to handle such amount of money. It's like having their little bodies crushed under a weight a hundred times greater than theirs. Their level of investment in self and personal development was way too incomparable to the level of money that appeared before them. So, to stay true to their correct financial state and mindset, and become comfortable, they have to let go of all the money one way or the other.

Yours might not be a lottery. In fact, you may even never experience something similar to a windfall in your whole life. But, if you don't invest in yourself and take personal development seriously, you'll end up like them. You might even be lucky with a certain real estate deal or key into a hot market and sell tons of info products that drops off some tens of thousand bucks in your account. But the bad side is that you will almost never be consistent doing it, or better still, you'll squander it away one way or the other. If the highest you ever made before was 120k per year, you'll never be comfortable until you have spent the money to reach that level.

And by saying you'll spend the money till it comes down to 120k, I don't necessarily mean lavish spending. In the examples of lottery winners I gave above, not all of them had the error of lavish spending. You might even give to foundations or charities like some of them did. You might start paying off some loans and debts that could wait few months more. You might start seeing that your kids and wife needs some more clothes, shoes and vacations. It's then you'll start to feel you have to change the four tires of your car to the one you saw advertised on TV as the best for the roads *(adverts you've always seen for the past six months)*. No matter how logical the spending is, they are, with a deeper look, never necessary and urgent. It's just self-sabotage. It's just your body's way of stabilizing you.

I'm sure you can relate this to your personal financial experience. This is real. What we eventually have in hand per time is often times the best we have ever handled in the past. Our mind always stays comfortable to whatever value our financial thermometer reads.

Do you know that Will Smith at some point owed the IRS 2.1 million dollars? Lady Gaga was technically bankrupt during her 2009 Monsters Ball tour. Mike Tyson filed for bankruptcy in 2003.

Donald Trump's companies have gone bankrupt more than six times. Despite once being rated as worth over $150 million, 50 cents filed for bankruptcy in 2015. Walt Disney was left bankrupt from his first film company. Abraham Lincoln paid off his debts until the 1840s, then became President in 1861. Larry King filed for bankruptcy the same year he was offered a national nightly television slot. Looking at the names involved, what would you say about them today? They are all national heroes, dead or living.

What do you think is the difference when you compare them to the list of those who lost their lottery windfalls? The difference is clear. The latter had the money they lost in the first place through sheer hard work and personal development. It came through the development and deployment of their talents, abilities, acumens, attitude, intelligence, among many other positive virtues. They deservedly made it and were involved in all the process. The most important thing was who they became in the process—a personality that bad habits, recession, 9/11 or whatever cannot take away from them. So, when they lost everything, all it took was for them to reach within them and reproduce it. So, what's the catch here?

It is that, to earn more, we must become more.

To join the 1 percent and become really, really, rich, you've got to become more. You see, money does not change you, but amplifies who you already are. If you are the spending type, it will only activate the spending demon in you. If you are the saving and investing type, you'll have more to do so. This is more reason we must always put personal development first. It is the way of the rich and wealthy.

It's always better big money better meets you mentally and emotionally prepared.

"We can't become what we want to be by remaining what we are."

\- Max DePree

In life, whatever we have not achieved or obtained through personal development will be hard to keep. You see, if someone hands you a million dollars, you'd better hurry up and become a millionaire. You'd better hurry up and become a man that can handle a million dollars. If not, you'll lose it. Tony Robbins said,

"If you took all the money in the world and divided it equally among everybody, it would soon be back in the same pockets it was before."

To have more than you've got, become more than you are.
This is what the focus of your attention should be, if not, the right quote for you would be: *Unless you change how you are, you'll always have what you've got.*

Let me give you a head start on why people hardly become rich in life. The reason is because of a simple fact they seem never to know: *To make more money, you have to become the type of person who makes more money.* There are an endless amount of tactics, strategies, and techniques for making more money. Some of them include freelancing, selling estates, asking for a raise, turning your hobby into a side-business, promoting other people's products, writing a book, creating an app, and blogging.

So, with so many ways to make money, why don't people make the amount of money that they want to be making?

Great question. The reason people don't make the amount of money that they want to make isn't because the opportunities for making more money don't exist or because their backs are so buried into the ground, but because they're not the type of person who is able to fully appreciate, and take advantage of, those opportunities.

Do you really understand that? Maybe I should rephrase it again for you.

The reason people don't make the amount of money that they want to make isn't because the opportunities for making more money don't exist, but because they have not trained themselves with the necessary mindset which helps them to identify, take advantage of, and maximize those opportunities. And because they are not ready for it, they self-sabotage in the face of a potentially life-changing opportunity to convince themselves that what is keeping them poor is probably some forces beyond their control.

They do things like the following:

When they notice an opportunity, they fail to act on it.

They decide that the opportunity is just too risky.

They start to act, but then they don't follow through.

To become the type of person who makes more money, you have to work on yourself.

> *"If you want to become successful, you must first become the person who can be successful."*
>
> **- Anonymous**

I can understand that, at this point, some might still have some problem trying to connect personal development to the amount of money they are earning or can earn. They'll still seem to ask questions like:

What does money have to do with my personal development? Everything. The answer is *"everything."*

Can you still imagine the example of the CEO and intern I shared earlier? The example teaches a basic lesson which is that: *We primarily get paid for the value we bring to the hour, not for the hour.* What this means is that if you work 8 hours, you don't get paid for 8 hours, you get paid for the value you bring in 8 hours, otherwise you might stay at home, do nothing and get paid. And why is it that more time won't help? It's because VALUE is what makes the difference in results. You can't always get more time, but you can create more value in the same time and get much money!

This all makes sense now, right?

Okay. If it's about VALUE, how is it possible?

If you are more valuable, the more your money becomes. And to be VALUABLE, it means you have to really work on yourself to become better than you have always been. It means you have to primarily work on yourself to become an above average person and you'll have an above average income. Your income always rises to the level of your personal investment in yourself. It's a direct connection. Arguably the greatest American business philosopher of all time, Jim Rohn, nailed it when he said: *"Work harder on yourself than you do on your job!"*. As you change or improve your philosophy, and better your attitude towards life, work, money and yourself, your financial outcomes automatically will match up positively.

So, if you want more money, it is clear you need to develop yourself. Thinking positive and saying daily affirmations are not the only actions needed. Work on yourself to bring more value on the marketplace and you will get more money.

Investing In Self Is the Secret of the Rich

How is it like when you want to get ahead in life and starting to make more money but with your same old body, brain, mind, and pretty everything else?

It's like attempting to drive a car without wheels. The engine will definitely rev, but there will never be any acceleration. When we fail to invest in ourselves and improve the quality of our lives so that we can be better mentally, emotionally, physically, psychologically, and spiritually each new day than before, we will never truly advance towards the direction of any dreams or goals in our mind.

In simple terms, personal development is a lifelong process of improving yourself in a way such that your lifestyle, future and personality become better than before. It is a sure vehicle for people to assess their skillsets and talents and set future goals in accordance to that, so that they constantly learn to become a better person than before. Any successful person you see today is someone who continuously works on his talent, skills, abilities, etc. and tries to improve and perfect them. On the other hand, unsuccessful people think the day graduation's over, learning surely is over.

"Personal development is the conscious choice to improve one's life to become a better person and to grow as an individual."

- **Anonymous**

Personal development is so crucial in your journey of wealth acquisition. Even if you had gone to college, personal development is still going to be what makes you above average and separate you from among your peers. For instance, let's consider two college graduates named Jeff and Jerry with the same educational qualification. Jeff has a hunger to learn, and the desire to improve himself which makes him to continuously learn new skills such as how to crack interviews, public speaking, communication skills, number of languages, investments, finances and other life skills. Jerry on the other hand is satisfied with his education qualifications and in turn didn't put much effort in acquiring any extra skills.

Out of the two, who do you think would get a better job, Jeff or Jerry? Imagine yourself as the Human Resource manager and interviewer, whose CV would you be fascinated with most and hire? *As a boss who would you prefer to give a higher salary?* If both of them couldn't get a job, who do you think has the more potential to cut it out quickly in the marketplace? I am sure your answers would be the same as mine. It's quite obvious, isn't it?

Personal development is what brings the edge factor between the two of them. Jeff would have all the confidence in this world because personal development will always keep him motivated to become a better person than before. Furthermore, it opens the doors for new and multiple opportunities for him than Jerry.

How to Develop Personally

Never stop to invest in yourself. You have to take personal development seriously if you must reach your financial goals. Personal development is a school that you can never graduate from. You must strive to become better than you were the day before you enter your grave. Warren Buffett, one of the wealthiest men that ever lived and one time richest man in the world says that the very best investment you can make is one that *"you can't beat, can't be taxed and one that not even inflation can take away from you."* He advocates that *"ultimately, there's one investment that supersedes all others: Investing in yourself. Nobody can take away what you've got in yourself, and everybody has potential they haven't used yet."* That is coming from a man considered by many as the greatest investment brain of this century.

> *"Investing in yourself is the best investment you will ever make. It will not only improve your life, it will improve the lives of all those around you."*
>
> -Robin Sharma

You cannot put a price on your investment in self-development. In return for all your efforts towards becoming better each day, you will always turn out a better, well-rounded personality, and attract more riches into your life. Never stop learning. Make kaizen your life watch. Adopt the virtue of constant and never-ending improvement. You will build your self-confidence and self-worth and acquire knowledge that places you far above your peers and competitors in the marketplace.

> *"Every time we push personal development aside, we invite personal struggle into our lives."*
>
> -Hal Elrod

How do you go about it?

There are many ways to do that. I'll start off the basics, one of which is cultivating a reading habit. By daily reading books of self-help, personal growth, and personal finance etc. you will tend to know the experiences of successful people, their rights and wrongs. You will learn about the path ahead, and what never to repeat including what to emulate. Moreover, it will keep you motivated, help you in finding your goals, purpose in life and useful wisdom of brilliant authors.

There are so many meaningful and wonderful books out there that you can read, that I'm sure will impact your life positively and set you on a trajectory to a life of abundance. There are also life-transforming podcasts you can listen to, and workshops to attend to learn from. How do you develop yourself and increase your knowledge from books, podcasts, videos, etc.? You develop yourself by making them a regular part of your life, consuming them in a measured, consistent fashion.

Read, or perhaps I should rephrase, listen to a book a week for the start. Like I wrote earlier, books or audio books are an infinite resource to building knowledge and expertise in any area. If you don't manage to read a book, quickly supplement your learning and curiosity with podcasts. If you think you don't have a curiosity to learn, just begin first at your speed. It's all about taking mini-steps that over time culminate into a bigger effect in results. *Listening to a 30-minute podcast before going to bed or when driving, or when working out in the gym is a great way to make effective use of time whilst still learning.*

Let me leak you another master secret. Use seminars and workshops a lot. Never miss them if it's along the area of your expertise. Use them to expand your knowledge and skills. Webinars, online classes and platforms like Udemy, Coursera, among others, are there to learn anything from. But the reason I'll love to sway towards seminars and workshops is the aspect of real human connection. You see, you will get to a level in life where you'll understand that relationship and network is everything. Doors that your intelligence, smartness, brilliance, skills, aptitude, among other great virtues cannot open, relationships do in a twinkle of an eye. A seminar event atmosphere gives you the invaluable opportunity to network with those who are like-minded. The right skill and help you need my just be three seats away from you.

Personal investment is an investment in your growth, awareness, and identity. It is what goes into you becoming a verse, well-rounded personality. It is not something only helps increases your life options, but the personage to respond and take advantage of them in a very responsible way. When you are giving to constant and never-ending learning and improvement, you will always have that competitive edge. You can't attend a good seminar and not come back without a new wave of ideas and inspirations. You probably know that already.

You Hold the Key to Your Success

If there's something I would say is a recurring theme in this book, it is the emphasis that you are the one in the driver seat of your life and no one can take your responsibilities for you. You are the only controller of yourself. Only you can take responsibility for your actions and allow yourself to be successful. I agree that support, encouragement, and mentorship from others are important, but you don't need to rely on them. You are first and foremost, the one who needs to make things happen for yourself, personally and professionally. Only you hold the key to your success so *make it happen.*

You hold the key to your success. The only approval you need is the one you give to yourself. So, give yourself permission. Ask yourself, what truly matters to you and what do you have a desire to live for? What do you want to accomplish? How do you want your financial destiny to end up? What do you want to be known for? How are you going to succeed?

Fix your eyes on the goal and never lose sight. See this moment an opportunity to better yourself. See it as the perfect opportunities for you to dare to dream, to test the waters, and to live your comfort zone. See it as an opportunity to stretch yourself, to meet new people and form alliances with like minds, and see as the first time you'll ever take your life absolutely gung-ho. See as this one time when nothing shall stand in the way of your desires and dreams no more.

"The biggest rewards in life are found outside your comfort zone. Live with it. Fear and risk are prerequisites if you want to enjoy a life of success and adventure."

- Jack Canfield

The journey starts for you today. Waiting for one to give approval or waiting for the perfect time will hold you back on achieving your goal of being successful. You might have to wait your whole life if that is the path you want to take. Remember your time is your life. It is valuable, so don't let another day pass without giving yourself permission to be successful. Value your life and acknowledge the talents that you have. Acknowledge the abilities and gifts that you possess. Surround yourself with people who will support your success. Those people should be encouraging you to be better and drive you higher every day. Keep those negative people away, don't let them discourage you from reaching your goal.

Prove to yourself that you can do it. Convince yourself. Take yourself by surprise with your actions. Create a positive life with small steps in the right direction. Step out of your comfort zone and into your courage zone and be confident about it. The goldmine you seek is not in the latest motivational speaker in town, the newest book on investing, or the most publicized seminar by a multimillionaire Internet marketer based in Las Vegas. It is you. You are the most important factor in what you need to become absolutely successful in life.

What is that thing you would have done all these years if you had no fear? The answer to that question is whatever fear has taken away from you. Face your fears. I love the way Susan Jeffers passed it across in her bestselling book, right from the title: *"Feel the Fear and Do It Anyway."* Many run from their fears instead of facing them. Fear is real, but your courage, persistence, and resoluteness are equally real. You are more capable of facing your fears than you may think. I have seen many definitions of the word FEAR. I've seen *False Evidence Appearing Real*. I've also seen *Forget Everything*

And Run and *Face Everything And Rise*. All these three, I believe, speak the same thing which is the encouragement that you should face your fears.

> *"What we fear doing most is usually what we most need to do."*
> - Ralph Waldo Emerson

Engage yourself in whatever works for you as regards personal growth. If it's Yoga, good. If it's meditation, equally fine. If it is between reading, praying, or exercising, the most important thing is that you do anything that will bring out the best in you. Throw those things that make you scared off the path and keep on going toward your success.

Only you, hold the key to your success.

You Want to Become Rich? Do These Things

The problem is that most people keep wishing that their circumstances would magically change for them. They don't have the desire or passion to become better themselves so they can proactively improve their own circumstances. While the world teems of many people like this, you can choose to be different and even a reference point for others by seeking to become the kind of person equipped with the skills and abilities to change the direction of his life, transform his life, and do brilliant things with it.

"The greatest reward in becoming a millionaire is not the amount of money that you earn. It is the kind of person that you are to become a millionaire."

- Jim Rohn
(Foremost American Business Philosopher)

You can become a problem solver, solution provider, and someone who does influential work in this world. To reach that quality as a person is something within your control. It's all tied to personal improvement and your ability to invest in yourself. You can't wish for it to happen. You must develop to becoming the kind of person who naturally attracts the success you seek.

Let me show you how through these simple but absolutely effective personal development life hacks:

Invest At Least 10 Percent of Your Income in Yourself

"To double your income and success, triple your investment in personal development and professional mastery."

- Robin Sharma

Do you know that if you don't pay for something, you rarely pay attention?

It is natural with us to want stuff for free. Internet marketers will always use any free things as a bait *(lead magnet)* to get your contact, most especially your email. But you would agree with me that you hardly take what is being sent to your mail serious. But if you had paid for it, you would quickly hit the complaint button when you don't see anything in your mail.

Anything we get for free; we don't take seriously.

So let me ask you this question: *How much do you invest in yourself? How committed are you to yourself?*

If you are not investing in yourself, that means you don't even care about what your life turns out to be. It means you can't even stake a bet on yourself. It means you are not even sure of your own ability to become successful.

It's a law of self-improvement that when you invest 10% of your income on yourself, will yield a 100X or more return on that investment. For every dollar you spend on your education, skills, refinement, and relationships, you'll get at least 100 dollars back in returns.

Whatever the figure is, let 10 percent of it go into your personal development. You may not have the money to hire a mentor or coach, but at least you can buy a book *(Just like you did by buying this one you are reading)*. How much money and time do you spend on entertainment, clothes, or groceries? It's a matter of priority.

If you want to do something extremely well, you need to make an investment in that direction. It's only when you invest in something that you have the motivation to make it happen. In life, your level of success can generally be measured by your level of investment. The reason you are not getting the results you want is because you haven't invested enough to get those results. Invest in books. Invest in online courses. Invest in seminars and workshops. Your personal investment will end up shaping many things in your life such as the quality of marriage and parent you'll become, the level of happiness you'll have, the quality of work you produce, and the weight of your riches.

When you spend on investing on yourself, you naturally become committed to yourself and your dreams. If you want a greater commitment, just invest more. You'll get to a point of no return and you'll become so passionately involved that withdrawing can never be an option. The moment you know what you want and why you want it *(not knowing could result in the problem of over-commitment to the wrong thing)*, you can begin to invest in that direction so as to get the maximum results out there.

Invest At Least 80 Percent of Your "Off" Time Into Learning

"Most people you see are consumers rather than creators. They are at work to get their paycheck, not to make a difference."

- Jim Rohn

See, for every time you spend on social media, you can't have it back, and that actually makes your future worse. Just like eating bad food, every consumed moment leaves you worse off. Every invested moment leaves you better off. I'm not saying you shouldn't do entertainment. A good music and comedy are sometimes great for the soul. But its better you be personal development conscious even in your desire to be entertained. Let it be the kind that leaves a positive impact on your relationships and other aspects of your life. Powerful documentaries can replace movies that makes no real impact on your life except a fun feeling. Entertainment can also be a powerful area where you deliberately invest in yourself. A good way to know if it was an investment is when that entertainment continues to yield returns over and over in your future. That may include positive memories, transformational learning, or deepened relationships.

Place entertainment alongside learning and education. Which one do you think will provide far greater returns in your future? You know the answer. You can't find a single successful person out there who doesn't read and take learning very seriously. Zimbabwean billionaire Strive Masiyiwa once said he was in a flight with Bill Clinton and when discussion takes them to any particular topic the next thing he hears is,

"what book are you reading about that?" Those are billionaires and they are still hanging on there through personal development.

How much more do you need?

Ultra-successful people understand that education and learning determine how well they see the world. They know that what they know determines the quality of the relationships they can have and the quality of work they can do. Don't forget the popular saying that, in the next few years, who you would have turned out to be will be as a result of the books you have read and the people you have moved with.

For all the "off" time you get, please pour as much of it as you can into learning and education of self. 80 percent of it is the recommended. Your input directly translates to your output. If you don't like the outcomes you are seeing in your life, you've got to change the input. What you put in is what you see come out. It is from the abundance of what you have in you that your words, actions, attitudes, philosophy, etc. comes out. Consuming junk media regularly isn't going to do your world any good.

It's simply garbage in, garbage out.

Work To Learn, Not For Money

This is one personal development hack that many won't understand if they can't see it at a deeper level. The temptation is to work for money and that is what poor people do. Wealthy and happy people work to learn. Unsuccessful and unhappy people work primarily for money. They trade their hours, energy, and strength for money.

Do you know the Pareto Principle? It says that it is only 20 percent of our efforts that actually guarantees 80 percent of the result we get. Going by this, I'll say only 20% of your energy should be spent doing your actual work. The rest should be spent learning, improving yourself, and resting. Yes, resting is critical.

When you dedicate all your time to doing a work and not only a portion of it, how are you going to become better at the work? If you are asked to cut down a tree in eight hours, wouldn't it be wise to spend the seven hours sharpening your saw? It is by *"sharpening your saw"* that you'll continue to become a better and more capable person. Let your greatest motivator in any endeavor be to learn and I assure you the knowledge gained will draw far more riches towards you.

Many people think lack of money is their problem, so they chase money. But if you chase money, it will grow wings and fly away. Instead of chasing, why not attract? And you can only do that by adding to your knowledge. When you prioritize learning and education over money in your work, you'll become a better thinker, communicator, and better at your craft, the quality of your work will continue to increase. During the hours you are actually working, you'll be in a deep flow state and connect seamlessly with your inner genius. You'll be absolutely focused, your mind stimulated, and never be distracted like most people are when they work. While working, you can get more done in a few hours than most people get done in a number of days. And eventually, you'll be able to charge really high fees for your work, because no one else can do it like you.

"Personal development separates you from the crowd."

Learn To Create More Value, And Not Just For The Sake Of It

"The key secret to success is not excessive expertise, but the ability to use it. Knowledge is worthless unless it is applied."

- Max Lukominskyi

One of the greatest ways to get the best out of your personal development efforts is learning to create more value and not just for the sake of it. There are a million things you could learn in this our media and information age, but if you don't put that learning into immediate practice, it becomes shallow *information*.

Focus on creating more value in your life and becoming better. Be committed to learning with great intensity and have the discernment to ignore almost everything while learning that which will bring the highest return. When you learn something, you should get a return on that learning. People that don't care about the returns are those who love entertainment and learning just for the sake of it. You must have met people like that before who read books now just to say they've read lots of books. Then what's the use of learning without application?

If you're not applying what you're learning, you are only consuming and wasting your time.

Set Aside At Least 10 Percent Of Your Income Into Stuff That Will Generate More Money

There are consumers and creators in this world, right?

It's absolutely your choice to become either of the two.

Very few people create true wealth. Most people you see who have high incomes are not truly wealthy. What they have is nothing but high incomes that equally goes down the drain through lavish and lascivious predilections. They go for a lifestyle that match their incomes. Their expenses always rise to cancel out their income. When they make more, they consume more. In fact, the reason most people make money solely is to consume.

Only very little people in this world make money to invest that money. How much of the amount you currently earn goes into any kind of investment?

The best time to start investing is now. Start today. Get yourself educated. Learn all you can. Create a vehicle, or several vehicles, where you regularly put at least 10% of your income. Eventually, as it has proven with so many successful people today, your investment vehicle may even start producing more profits for you than your actual business.

Remember the power of compound interest. If you put 10% of your income into your investments over a long enough period of time, you'll be very alright at the end of the day. You'll be able to stop working and retire anytime you really feel like.

Shift From Being A Getter to A Giver

Please I beg you never to be like most people who are only focused on what they can get out of life. Their *all-the-time* language is me, me, and me. Their attention is only on what they can get and not what they can give. You know what?

"Me" only makes you think of yourself and family. Meanwhile, successful people think about providing solutions to the problems of many by creating products and services. They think beyond meeting their own and their immediate family's needs. They think about the needs of the world or a group of people beyond themselves.

"The world gives to the givers and takes from the takers."

-Joe Polish

Think of Steve Job's Apple. Think of Mark Zuckerberg's Facebook and WhatsApp. Think of Jeff Bezos' Amazon. Think of Jack Ma's Alibaba and Aliexpress. Think of Bill Gates' Microsoft. Think of Colonel Sander's KFC. Think of Napoleon Hill's "Think and Grow Rich." Think of Michael Jackson's "Thriller" track.

Then think about you!

Is there anything you have ever done with your life with the mindset of reaching a wide audience of people? Any product or service you ever created with the mindset of it providing solutions to many people's problem whether at local, national, or international level?

The reason you are poor is because you think only about yourself.

Your small-mindedness is your demon. Once you become more consciously awake to the world, your desire will shift from merely receiving to giving. You will think in terms of contribution, not acquisition. You'll think in terms of giving, and not just taking. You'll realize that it's actually far more satisfying to give than to get.

This hack might be all that you'll need to hear through this book.

When you open your mind as to what you can give, a single idea can be all that will do the magic. Shift your mindset to giving. Surround yourself with fellow givers and resent takers like a plague. When your motivation is to give, you'll often get insights into how you can improve your relationships and deepen ideas about how you can improve other people's lives and transform their businesses will come handy to you.

I repeat: *This hack might be all that you'll need to hear through this book.* You'll start contributing more. You'll become a creator because your mind is open to other people's problems. Far more opportunities than you can probably handle will come at your direction because the world now loves and trusts you to come to its aid. Above all, you'll become far more inspired and impactful.

Acknowledge That You Need Others To Thrive

You need the help of others to achieve anything in this world. Show me any successful person and I will show you someone who have leveraged on the strength of people around him. Likewise, show me a failure and I will show you someone who has nobody to learn from.

Just because you have steadied your mindset at being a giver and not a taker doesn't mean you don't also seek a lot of help. In reality, you are constantly seeking and receiving help. No one can survive in this world, personally or professionally, without depending on other people to do what only they can do best. But it takes wisdom and humility to openly acknowledge this dependence because many see it as weakness, but really, it's a strength.

On the road to your financial goal, don't just be keen at acknowledging your dependence. Build up the habit of constantly expressing your *appreciation* to the people in your life.

I love the way Michael Fishman captured it brilliantly:

"Self-made is an illusion. There are many people who played divine roles in you having the life that you have today. Be sure to let them know how grateful you are."

You are relationships away from achieving your goals. You are a relationship away from living the life of your dreams. You are a relationship away from starting to make the kind of money you want to be making.

Settle On What "Wealth" And "Success" Means To You

Do you know that success and wealth are not all about money? If it were all about money, all I will talk about in this book will be getting your 300k goal and nothing else. Then you can go ahead and waste it, squander it, and never learn other key things in your financial journey that will make you a well-rounded man.

See, there are a lot of people who have money and have little *"capital"* in the other key areas of their lives. I don't ever want you to become like such people.

I want you to make the money, save it, grow it, invest it, spend it, enjoy it, and do great things in life with it, but all these shouldn't come at the expense of your relationships, spirituality, personal integrity, health and wellness, among many others.

Obviously, money is very important. It makes the world go round. The bible calls it a "defense". It solves a lot of problems. It speeds processes. But know this also: *Money is nothing but a tool. It's not the end, but a means to it. It is a means of contributing to your world and make it a better place.* You may not turn out very wealthy at the end of your life for just having *"money"* only. At that point, you'll finally realize that relationships and health are also forms of wealth. It'll be a shame indeed to read this book from start to finish and still turn out to be like a man called very rich for only having money.

You need to define and settle on whatever wealth, money, and success means to you so that you won't make 300k and the first thing coming to your mind is to google the price of the latest Bugatti out there and an exquisite bungalow in Manhattan.

Know Your "Why" And Let it Drive You

> *"He who has a 'why' to live can bear almost any how"*
>
> - Fredrick Nietzsche

Why do you really want to become rich?

Is it so that you can lead a better life? Is it because you want a better life for your kids? Is it because you want to live in opulence?

Whatever your reason is, if your *"Why"* is not strong enough, you'll get tired along the way. When your "Why" is very strong, you'll turn out a completely different animal in the pursuit of your goals. You'll be invested in anything you have to do to achieve it.

You'll be totally motivated to pursue it and you'll challenge yourself to pull it off.

No, will never be an answer. Until you get a Yes.

Reflections

- How do you personally understand and interpret the statement: *"Income rarely exceeds personal development"*?
- What do you think is the reason most lottery winners always end up broke?
- *"To earn more, we must become more."* What message do you think this statement is passing to you particularly?
- Do you agree that money doesn't really change you but only amplifies who you have always been?
- What do you personally understand by the word *"Value"* and *"Personal Development?"*
- What are those things you'll start doing or improve upon to improve yourself personally?
- Which of the 9 hacks speaks to you the most personally and hits an area where you have really messed up? What do you resolve to do instantly to show that you have changed your mind about it and ready to move in the right direction?

CHAPTER 7

Understanding The Money Game

"When I was young I thought that money was the most important thing in life; now that I am old I know that it is."

Oscar Wilde.

Money really is a strange concept. You see those who do not have it aiming for it with all their strength and you see many of those who have it full of trepidations. Sometimes it's the most beautiful thing in the world to behold. Sometimes, it's more like a poisoned chalice.

But really, what is money?

It is hard to define money and agree on a singular definition of it. To some, it is a source and sustainer of happiness. There are others that believe it is a tool to control and dominate. There are still some that see it as a means to do good in this world. There are many mindsets and definitions to what money really is. But if we can really understand what it is, we will make our lives much easier.

Now, let me give you a definition I really want you to stick with for the rest of your life. Why would I want you to stick with it? The reason is because the definition is right from personal development playbook. Remember that your income always rises to your level of personal development and that we can only earn more when we become more.

Follow me.

In life, you can become rich through many means. Two are common. You either make money by devoting most of your time to a moneymaking venture or, you can wait many years and be rich by saving a percentage of your income, leaning on the power of compound interest.

When you devote your time and energy to a moneymaking venture, you have something you are offering or selling to the public and you get money in return, right? When you save, all you have is all that you have kept, right? This is why most people don't become rich by saving or cutting down expenses. You become rich by increasing your income to the extent that it makes your responsible expenses becomes irrelevant. I'll still come to that. Let's focus on moneymaking ventures for now.

When you make money by working at your job or business, it's a value you are creating for your employer or customers. You are creating something they deemed worthy, something they need and are willing to have and give back to you something in return. What you offer is VALUABLE to them and what you earn from them is the exchange for providing this value.

If you want to make a hundred thousand dollars in X amount of time, ask yourself how to create a value worth a hundred thousand dollars in X amount of time. Don't think in terms of how you can get a hundred thousand dollars in currency notes. When you stop thinking about currency notes you will automatically stop thinking about lottery, gambling and penny stock, for example. In all those three, you only make or lose money and no value is created.

Maybe you too have pondered on buying penny stocks in the past, those which would grow into a giant corporation and render you a couple million dollars in profit. I'm sure by now you know that was just ridiculous thinking on your part. Such only happens in dreams and to filthy lucky ones in real life.

Maybe you've even fantasized about lotteries before. Well, you know how the statistics of lottery winners look like. Some people do win it, as some do inherit real estates too, and there are others with claims of making huge sums in stock market gambling as well. These are one-off cases and can never be sustainable. Even if you win a lottery, the chance that you'll repeat the feat again is close to zero and there is no guarantee you won't end up like those in the past. Shouldn't we look past waiting for a windfall and focus on a way to make sustainable income? As simple as it sounds, for you to make $100, you need to create value of $100. There is no easier way of making money and becoming rich than that.

Why?

Because *money is value!*

People often ask: *how do I make money? How do I become wealthy? What's the secret to becoming wealthy? How do I get a high-paying job? How do I ask for a raise at work?*

These are all important questions. But the answer to them is nothing complex as people might think it is. In order to build wealth one way or the other, you must first create value. That is what the money you seek for is tied to.

You cannot have the first without the second. You cannot have money without creating value.

Now, you might ask: *"What is value?"*

"Value" is defined as an item that is something *"of worth, importance, or merit."* However, this definition doesn't even begin to scratch the surface of what the true meaning of value is.

From one individual to the other, **"Value"** may have a different definition but in terms of creating wealth and success, value is precious, has tangible worth and is sought after.

Think for a moment. Picture the most important item that you have ever purchased for yourself. How expensive was it? You most likely didn't mind that you worked long hours, even overtime, to get the money, and it never really bothered you that you had to even cut down on additional expenses to obtain that item. To you, it was precious, had tangible worth and was sought after. The price didn't matter. The *"Value"* you think the item is bringing into your life is all you can see right in front of you. You paid the money by the way.

That's the way it works with value and money. *Money is the currency in which people pay for value.* Knowing this truth gives you the answer the most fundamental and functional answer to your questions about money and wealth.

This is the definition I want to stick with you for the rest of your lives, that *money is value*. This is how the universe works. Without this, we can never maintain the natural order.

Human being created currency notes, meant to be a medium of exchanging values between people. Health is a value. Home is a value. Great food is a value. Nice suit is a value. Ideas and skills are values. Private jet is value. Music is value. Money is value. To oscillate between all these different kinds of values, money is mostly at the center. Money is what we exchange for most of these things. When value changes position, money always replaces it.

You need to really understand this. It's the greatest thing you'll have to understand about the game of money.

Once again, let it stick: *Money is value!*

To make money, the formula is pretty simple: To earn $X, create $X value. Can you please name me someone who's known for his monetary wealth and not for his value creation? Is it Rockefeller, Gates, or Colonel Sanders?

Or Steve Jobs? Or Oprah?

Rockefeller, America's first billionaire is more regarded for his oil business. At a point in time, *Wikipedia* started about him on their page like:

"*Rockefeller revolutionized the petroleum industry and defined the structure of modern philanthropy.*" That was mentioned at the beginning of the page before his wealth was mentioned. What about Gates, Jobs, Oprah, and Sanders? Bill Gate made the computer something the average man could possess. Steve Jobs revolutionized the phone industry with Apple. Sanders changed the way chicken is prepared and developed a league of raving customers. Oprah created a show that everyone wouldn't want to miss. These are people who created tremendous value in our lives. They didn't win lottery or gambled in stock market. They made a fortune by creating enormous value.

Rockefeller has been long dead but the value he created is still in our world today, so is Steve Jobs and Colonel Sanders. Do you know what your last test of how you've lived your life would be? It won't be about how much money you have in the bank. Your success will be measured by how many people love you and how much value you created for them.

The more the value you create for others, the richer you'll become in the long run. It will take time and effort to spread the message of the value you are creating *(selling and marketing)*. Once it's out, so long the value created is a solution that people need in scores, there's no stopping to the height you can reach. Regardless of what you want to do in life, there is no limit to how much you can earn. Creating value to create a solid financial future is independent of a set path. The revenue-generation potential is independent of what you do. It has nothing to do with how lucrative the career path or kind of business you do is. You can sell cufflinks and become a millionaire within a year if you optimize things well while you can also start out in the seemingly-lucrative real estate industry and yet make less than $200k in your first two years. Many of us see drawing and painting as a hobby that would hardly earn any money, but the top artists earn more money than we can ever imagine. The singular thing that matters and that determine your wealth is how much value you're bringing to the world.

This truth is same for many other professions out there, be it teaching, sports, acting, racing, fitness, videography, photography, computer programming, creative writing, virtual assistance, and so on. It's all about the value you can create for the outside world. As long as you create value, people will pay money for it. People are literally going all about with their hard-earned money and will only part away with it for anything their judgment, logical or emotional, says it's worth it. That is where you come in. To get the money, you don't focus on the money.

Rather, you focus on the value.

I hope you've seen again, more clearly, that *money is value*.

This is what understanding the money game really is about. See, there are many schools of thoughts to making money, but I am not here to share them. What I have business with is showing you an angle about money that helps you with the right mindset which translates to you achieving your financial goals in the easiest and most effective way possible. And to that effect, all you need to know is that money is value. Once you master this singular idea about money, it changes your financial world.

In the world of making money, to make $X, you need to generate a product or service that someone else wants to have for $X. To make $300k, you need to generate a product or service that someone else wants to have for $300k. For instance, if it's a great product worth $5, to hit your target, you've got to persuade about 60,000 people through whatever ethical means to buy it. Let's say it's a phenomenal service worth $50 in value, you'll have to convince 6,000 people to buy into it.

How can you create this $X of value for others for you to make $X amount must become the most important question you start to ask yourself?

Whether this value creation comes from selling a product or a service, or even a bright idea; it's all great. Even if it means you are going to do Santa Claus in 10 cities within 2 days, so long you have not involved in gambling or anything unethical, you are creating value. Look at what Michael Zuckerberg did. He saw value in providing people *(social animals)* an online social atmosphere, and that value addition changed our lives forever. Look at Elon Musk, Peter Thiel, and co. They saw the need for money to be transferred easily from one end of the world to the other and ease people's money concern, hence the emergence of PayPal. Sarah Blakely's Spanx came out of nowhere and changed the game by creating a new kind of underwear that men and women will wear with ease, comfort, and a smile on their faces.

If you want to make money, start thinking what can you do to help change others' lives for the better? The more value you create, the more money you'll make. The more you can enhance their lives, the more they'll want to pay. The more problem you solve, the more the money you make. To make a million dollars, you've got to solve a million-dollar problem. To make 200k a year, you've got to solve or meet the need of a 200k project within the time frame. That is the only way.

Change your thoughts about making money. Relax your mind and think about ways to achieve your financial goals. Start by first thinking in terms of the value that you are going to create for takers.

Think about how you can create value worth $100,000. Don't think about

"How can I make $100,000?"

At this point can you take a piece of paper and write down this question for yourself. How much do I really want to earn or be earning *(what's my financial goal)?*

Let's say it's 100k. To help your mind see it as something not too big, you can say, making 9 thousand dollars a month. Having identified the goal, the next thing for you is to start building your self-awareness. This means you have to stop seeing this goal as a monetary, financial goal.

Rather, start seeing it in terms of the value you need to create. The last step is the *"how"*. You must settle on how do you intend to create this $100,000 of value for others? Think of as many ways as possible.

Let me help you with some quick questions to narrow the search: Who are the people you need to create value for? And what are the biggest needs of those people?

What needs of your target population are not met by others before you?

What are you better at doing that you can offer?

What will be most *(or more)* beneficial to others?

How can you make them aware of your work toward their benefits? Do you need external help? Where can you get help?

Make More Value, Not Money

Let's say you wake up this morning, get dressed, and step out to take a taxi to a conference. You behold the taxi driver and he was very polite. The taxi was clean, and the driver takes you directly to your destination. In all, it was good service, and you paid him about $10.00 for the value that he created. I call this level 1 value creation. It's a commodity and any other reasonable taxi driver would have done as well for exactly the same money. The third day, you stepped out of the hotel to a different experience. A tall, handsome looking man, dressed in a tuxedo, approached, soft-spoken, and said "Excuse me, sir, are you going to get a taxi?" You said, "Yes", and then he asked: "Would you consider taking a town car for $80?" That's a little more than a taxi, but you assumed it was also going to be a better experience. You gave it a try. Soon, he had returned in a nice Mercedes Benz. He took your luggage.

He had an unread copy of the newspaper on the seat, a couple bottles of cold water in the cup holders, and also had a couple magazines in the back of the front seat. He was super polite, smart, and funny and he offered to play your favorite songs if you wouldn't mind during the short trip. You loved every bit of it. You even gave him a $30 tip for a good work done. That was a better experience for what you'll call a level 2 value creation.

What is the difference between these two taxi drivers? They make different amount of money, right? But that's not actually what is different about them. The second taxi driver's value creation made him worth paying more to, and that's the reason you gave him a good tip for his effort in making your trip a better experience. To make the same amount or even greater money, the first driver needs to ask himself some very simple questions:

What can I do to make myself worth paying more to?

What could I do for my clients that make you more valuable?

What is that single thing I can change about myself and my business that'll shoot up my value?

What could you do that would allow you to create a greater level of value and make it difficult for your competitors to duplicate?

Even if they can duplicate every other thing, what is the human factor I can bring to the table that becomes my unique value point, something which knocks them off and makes you the go-to guy.

The truth is this. We all want more money. But no matter how much money we have, we always want more. You must have thought to yourself in the past something like: if I wanted to be happier, I needed to earn more money. But in reality—the only way you'll become happier is to create more value to others and be more useful to others. Also, when it comes to money and wealth, the only way to become richer is to create more value for others. Because the more value you create for others, the more valuable you become. Then the more valuable your services are, the more valuable your influence.

You might have been taught some other ways of making money and becoming richer. But today, as you read this book you will discover the politically incorrect truth about money. Your dad and mum will probably disagree with it. Of course, let them. They are wonderful set of people, but truth is if they know about how to make money so well, and teach you at a very young age will you be where you are today?

Now see the truth. Pinching pennies is a losing game. Obsessing about cutting costs is a waste of your valuable time and energy. You will eventually lose in the money game if all you do is spend your life this way. You see, the only way to truly create financial independence and take control of your future is by adding value to the world and creating your own economy. You don't build wealth by extreme cost cutting. Not at all. It encircles you in all manners of negativity. Instead, you build wealth by increasing your income, so you have much more money to save and invest.

Can you read that again? *You don't build wealth by extreme cost cutting and saving.* Now isn't that all you've been taught before.

Think. How much will you save per day to ever make a million dollars? Maybe a thousand years considering where you currently are at.

"But right now, all I can do is try to cut expenses." I understand you. Many of us have been there before. But unfortunately, saving and cost cutting can only keep you a bit warm, not hot. You can do all the cutting and slashing to the bone but there is nothing you can do about the bone.

What do I mean by the bones? You have to eat. You must pay rent. Emergencies will always come up. These are necessary spending and there is nothing you can do about them.

Let me make this a bit more practical for you.

Let's say you have an income of $40,000 per year. Someone making that amount of money in US, with no dependent, would be getting about $600 per week in take-home pay. Now let's put your monthly expenses as $600 for rent, $300 for transportation, and $300 for food. You're left with $1200 per month for everything else. You and I know that there are many other things in-between. But let us just agree for the sake of example that the remaining is $1200.

But wait, there's more. The universe has its own way of doing things. A spouse, girlfriend, child, even a pet, are all that it throws at us with the financial responsibilities that comes with it. I hope you know that quality dog and cat food cost no meagre fee.

Now things start to become really tight. And that leaves you with two choices. It's either for you to put your positive energy into earning more money or exhaust yourself with the negative mindset of cutting costs. You can only do one or the other. Please read and read again this quote below by New York Times bestselling author **Ramit Sethi:**

"We have limited cognition and attention, so each additional thing we try to focus on means an overall reduced amount of willpower and attention."

Do you know what that quote means? It means when you take the option of cutting cost and saving all you have; it weakens your willpower and attention to actually making sure that you increase your income. Answer this question: If you had to use your limited willpower to cut back on $2 a day of something you love, versus learning how to learn a skill on Udemy that will add up to $2000 to your income, which would you rather do?"

Exactly the answer in your mind right now: That's what I will do too.

So, please stop trying to cut costs to the bone.

You are cold, fine. You are afraid, fine. You feel like it's tough to take, expected. But I'm showing you the way in this book, so I want you to trust me. So, take all the energy that you put into slashing your budget and transfer it over to creating value and you'll become rich for it.

It will make all the difference in the world to your wealth building efforts. It's easier to make money than it is to slash expenses. I have shown you the equation of making money already the same way you have the quadratic equation in mathematics. It's simply:

Money = Value.

So, to make MORE money, all you need to do is take your skills, add the way you create value and do it for more people. It's all about adding more value.

It's not rocket science. That's it.

Add more value = make more money.

The best thing for you to do if you need more money is to switch from a negative cost-cutting mindset to a positive value-adding approach. When you need money, the right thinking is to find a way to make more of it. You can only slash your spending so far. Sooner than you expected you'll hit the bone of necessity and that'll be a brick wall. You can never cut through that.

So how do you now make more? You need to switch your energy over to creating more value.

You hear stuff like: making money is hard. The rich lifestyles are shady. You better clip coupons and drive an extra mile to save on gas. Cut down on groceries and plant a garden in your backyard instead.

This is all wrong approach.

Please show me any millionaire or billionaire you know of that has lived life this way. Or show me a neighbor of yours that is ahead of you financially who lives this way. That approach is WRONG.

It keeps your mind focused on want, needs, and scarcity. It keeps your mind closed. It makes your mind stayed on just yourself instead of reaching out to the world.

That is the way the 96 percent are programmed to think and live life. Why would you go that path when you can add value to the world through your gifts, business, skills, ideas, etc. and make it a better place, AND make more money ALL at the same time.

Why not choose to become a person of value.

And as you work more on your value, knowing that income rises to the level of your personal development, you become richer and make more money.

Please focus on becoming a person of value.

If you want to earn more money in life, think about how you can be more valuable in life— rather than how you can make more money. Expand wealth for everyone.

Think to yourself— *"How can I create more wealth and value for other people?"* By focusing on others *(rather than yourself);* you start to really think of how you can be best useful to others. Can You Sell?

"The ability to sell is the number one skill in business. If you cannot sell, don't bother thinking about becoming a business owner."

- Robert Kiyosaki

It doesn't matter what industry you're in or what your business idea is all about.

You must be able to sell.

This is the one thing all successful people know how to do well. Without this skill, you won't succeed.

Please don't believe anything contrary to this!

I once saw a report where about 20 business owners and CEOs where asked to name the one skill they feel contributes the most to their success. Every one of them said *sales skills*. They all felt success is almost impossible—in any field—without solid sales skills.

To many people, the word selling means manipulating, pressuring, and sweet-talking. But if you think of *selling* as explaining the logic and benefits of a decision, then everyone, business owner or not, needs sales skills. Whatever your value proposition is, you'll need to convince others that your idea makes sense, show investors or bosses how a project or business will generate massive return, and help employees understand the benefits of a new process, etc.

In reality, sales skills are nothing but communication skills. Communication skill is something very critical in any business or career and you'll learn more about communication by working in sales than you will anywhere else. If your idea involves starting an SME or a company around your products or services, gaining sales skills will help you win financing, bring in investors, line up distribution deals, and land customers.

In business, everything involves sales and revolves around sales.

As you can see, the most talented artist doesn't always end up as the richest. It is the one that can come up with the best-selling strategy and can find a way to convince people that whatever he/she offers is worth buying into. Regardless of your skills, gifts, or talents, spending time investing in selling skills is an investment that will pay dividends forever. If it is real estate, you'll have to crack the fundamentals of land and properties selling. If it is ecommerce, you'll have to master online selling skills. If you decide to make your money through your writing gifts, you'll have to learn how to *"write in a persuasive way that sells"*. Even if all you have is your ability to paint or sing, you still cannot get the highest equivalent in financial rewards if you are devoid of good selling skills.

The most successful preachers around, as much as you know, are those who can eloquently communicate their visions and command the master ability to sell it, including their personalities. The greatest of all leaders like Luther, Mandela, Gandhi, among others are those who could articulate their passion and sell their messages to their followers convincingly. The biggest and ultra-successful brands, like Walmart, McDonald, and Uber, among others, spend a fortune to acquire a customer. They will do anything to ensure that a customer makes a buying decision very easily.

They focus massively on sales.

It's hard to succeed at whatever you do if you don't have sales skills.

Know this:

whatever you do or offer to the world, you are always selling.

You have to sell yourself, your products and your ideas constantly. You have to influence those around you to take action about whatever value you are offering, or you won't get very far. Even if the path you want to take to achieve your money goal is to get a higher paying job, you'll still be required to sell the hiring manager on why you are the right candidate. If you want it through a raise or promotion, you are selling them on why you earned it.

If you are married right now, it is because you were able to persuade your husband or wife to marry you. I'm sure that in the past you have had to persuade your friend to go see a movie or follow you to see a match.

Selling is something we all do naturally, but we can all improve on it. Improving on just this skill alone is enough to break anyone away from the shackles of poverty and plant their feet on the road to enduring wealth.

From the beginning of this book, you must have seen my passion to tell you the way things are.

Why?

Because I don't want this to be the next book you'll read and just toss over the shelf or leave somewhere in the corner of your laptop. I want it to inspire your life and help you achieve your financial goal. I want it to help you break out of a poverty rut.

You want success? Love to Sell. That is the answer.

You want to reach your financial goals? Love to Sell. That is the answer. You want to make 300k a year even without a college degree? Love to Sell. That is the answer.

This is the one characteristic that unites all highly successful people and you must adopt it. It's the way of the 99 percent. They love to sell. No idea, expertise, product or service ever became successful without somebody selling it to investors, peers, employees and customers.

It is the big secret of success. You must enjoy selling.

Understanding the sales process, and how to build long-term customer relationships, is incredibly important to you raising the kind of money you want to raise, and not just raising it, but keeping the flow of more of it into your life on a consistent level.

There are amazing benefits you get when you master the ability to sell and they not only serve you for the purpose of reaching your financial goals. They serve you in the long run as they become part of you. When you learn and give yourself to selling skills, you'll improve your negotiating ability. There is no enterprise on earth that doesn't involve negotiating: with customers, with vendors and suppliers, even with employees. Someone given to selling skills naturally learns to listen, evaluate variables, identify key drivers, overcome objections, and find ways to reach agreement without burning bridges.

Another great benefit of giving yourself to mastering the skill of selling is that you'll learn to close. Whatever the amount of money your financial goal reads, it is in the hand of others and you'll have to make them want and decide to give you. Asking for what you want is difficult for a lot of people. Closing a sale is part art, part science. Getting others to agree with you and follow your direction is also part art and part science. If your product is worth $20, you've got to convince people to agree with you that the value is worth that much. But that isn't enough. You must go further to have them enter their card details and part with the money. Now, that is closing, and it is only when you get into the art of selling that you master it.

Being given to selling, you'll also learn the spirit of persistence. Salespeople hear the word *no* all the time. People disagree with your valuation of a product or services and raise one objection or the other. But over time you'll start to see no as a challenge, not a rejection. You'll learn to take people over the finishing line. You'll learn to counter every objection and shape people's buying decision towards your brand. And you'll smile to the bank for it.

Can you sell? Because if you cannot you'll hardly master self-discipline which is a crucial component of personal development. If you work on a job, there are times when you sleepwalk your way through a day many times and still get paid. But when you are doing your thing, you know the foundational belief has got to be *"if it is to be, it's up to me."* You know you'll have to work your socks off and make sales happen. You won't be ever comfortable seeing those inventories overstaying their time in the garage. You won't be ever comfortable having your stock near full and unsold. You take responsibility for everything. In your mind, you have connected the dots between performance and reward. You ensure that you make the sales happen and keep the flow of money coming in.

Can you sell? If you can or commit to mastering it, you have discovered a perfect cure for shyness. You naturally gain confidence whether you are selling to people face to face or you are operating behind a computer. You'll gain more confidence and assuredness in your ability to pull stuff off even under duress or crisis. Working in sales is the perfect cure for shyness. You'll learn to step forward with confidence, especially under duress or in a crisis.

I bet it with you that right now, part of the reason you're struggling is probably because of poor sales skills.

Every successful business owner out there spends the majority of their time *"selling."*

Go learn how to sell.

It's the best investment you will ever make.

This is also all about being committed to personal development and learning to become a person of value. The more value you can bring to a large number of people, the more money you make in the process. And the more you can master the skill of selling anything, the richer you'll also become.

By now, if you have put to great use all that I have shown you, you should be a money magnet by now. You should be able to attract success, people, and the resources you need into your life because money/ wealth flows in the direction of value.

But how do you create value and get paid for it and make money.

You must find an outlet.

By outlet, I mean a vehicle or channel through which money flows to you. It is through it that your skills are being substantiated into money. Some call it niches. Some call industry. Some call it gifts. Some call it potential. Whatever the word used, they all remain channels through which you exchange skills, knowledge, wisdom, etc. for the monetary equivalents. It could be real estate. It could be trading crypto currency. It could be through ecommerce. It could be a soap making business. It could be blogging or copywriting. It could be from trading the stock markets. It could be playing the piano. It could be football. It could be from service business. And many others.

You must find one of these outlets that relates to your area of expertise, skills, knowledge, or interest. By interest I mean you may have no particular skill right now that you could offer as value in exchange for money but that does not stop you from playing the money game. You can learn as fast as you want to so long you are committed to succeeding in that particular endeavor.

"Everyone is an entrepreneur. The only skills you need to be an entrepreneur: an ability to fail, an ability to have ideas, to sell those ideas, to execute on those ideas, and to be persistent so even as you fail you learn and move onto the next adventure."

From the Bottom

- James Altucher

Find Your Value!

Of all things I have explained in this book, one of the chief things I'd also like you to remember forever is that everyone is born with a gift. I'm not going to be spending time here to be explaining to you what a *"gift"* means. I believe enough has been written about that already in books all around.

All I want to impress on your heart is the fact that your gift is a value. If you agree that your gift is a value then it's a ticket out of a life of lack and extreme poverty.

This is the reason I did not start talking about either money or gifts because the rich do not see it that way. I rather write about investing in yourself and I'm sure you got the point.

Upgrade your skills. Please do all you can to hone your skills and never relent in refining your craft.

If you have the natural ability to sing, nobody will gather in stadiums to watch you or buy your album if you cannot train that voice into something more sonorous. If you are blessed with a great height and you love playing basketball, you are a disciplined coach away from making your life count and earning huge money. If you are blessed with an eye for perspective, your paintings could soon be selling at a million dollars each.

There are just too many gifts out there that if honed and shared with the world, it will be a great blessing and of course, fortunes will be made as a result.

Whatever you are good at doing is also a value.

Your skill is a value. The faster you understand this, the better.

No one is without any kind of abilities.

Reflections

- For you, what is money?
- From personal experiences, how do you connect money and value?
- Do you believe in getting rich by cutting expenses? Have you tried that in the past and did it work for you?
- From your understanding of this chapter, what do you think has changed about the way you have always thought and understood money?
- On the scale of 1 to 10, what do you think your selling skills is at?
- Before reading this chapter, have you always known from a practical and personal point of view the importance of selling skills in a business? If yes, what additional things did you learn after reading it?
- Do you agree that investing in selling skills is the best investment you can make for your business?

References

Chapter 1

Reijman, Mark. "Why the Rich Stays Rich and The Poor Stays Poor." The Star Online, 17, June, 2017, https://www.thestar.com.my/business/business-news/2017/06/17/why-the-rich-stay-rich-and-the-poor-stay-poor

"What Is The Current Poverty Rate in the United States?" *UC Davis Center for Poverty Research*, https://poverty.ucdavis.edu/faq/what-current-poverty-rateunited-states

"Global Wealth Report 2018: US and China in the lead." *Credit Suisse*, 18 Oct. 2018, https://www.credit-suisse.com/about-us-news/en/articles/news-and-expertise/global-wealth-report-2018-us-and-china-in-the-lead-201810.html# Boghani, Priyanka. "How Poverty Can Follow Children Into Adulthood." *Frontline*, 22 Nov. 2017, https://www.pbs.org/wgbh/frontline/article/how-poverty-can-follow-children-into-adulthood/

"How To Escape the Poverty Trap for Good." *The Guardian*, https://www.theguardian.com/advertiser-content/stand-together/how-to-escape-the-poverty-trap-for-good

Mencimer, Stepahnie. "If You're Born Poor, You'll Probably Stay That Way." *Motherjones*, https://www.motherjones.com/politics/2014/06/the-long-shadow-poverty-baltimore-poor-children/

Chapter 2

Bartkiw, Esther. "One Percent of the People Makes 96 Percent of the Money." *Selfgrowth*, https://www.selfgrowth.com/articles/one_percent_of_the_people_make_96_of_the_money.html

Chapter 3

Weissmann, Jordan. "53 Percent of Recent College Grads Are Jobless or Unemployed—How?" *The Atlantic*, 23 April 2012, https://www.theatlantic.com/business/archive/2012/04/53-of-recent-college-grads-are-jobless-or-underemployed-how/256237/

McWhinnie, Eric. "College Grads: Overqualified and Unprepared?" *USA Today*, 24 May, 2013, https://www.usatoday.com/story/money/business/2013/05/24/college-grads-unprepared/2350633/#:

"How School Trains Us To Fail in the Real World." *Stephen Guise*, https://stephenguise.com/how-school-trains-us-to-fail-in-the-real-world/

Patel, Sujan. "7 Reasons You Don't Need a College Degree to Earn Big." *Inc.*, https://www.inc.com/sujan-patel/7-reasons-you-dont-need-a-college-degree-to-earn-b.html

Chapter 6

Genig, Hannah. "Out of Luck: Lottery Winners Who Have Gone Bankrupt." *Msn.com*, 28 Oct., 2018, https://www.msn.com/en-us/money/news/out-of-luck-lottery-winners-who-have-gone-bankrupt/ ar-BBP0F81

About the Author

Tonyell Toliver is a master's level social worker (MSW, CSW) with many years of experience. Toliver attended Warren Easton Fundamental Senior High School where she played several musical instruments. She earned herself a scholarship to Grambling State University, and she bagged a degree in social work in the summer of 2000. She has worked with a lot of people with challenging, financial situations. Toliver was raised by her single mother, and an older brother in an impoverished housing development neighborhood known as Calliope Project in New Orleans, Louisiana. She knows how terrible poverty is because she was born and raised in it. She spent so many years avoiding social work until her advice changed people lives for the better. Her life and her experiences are summed up in this book to help people get out of poverty. Toliver's passion as a social worker has propelled her into becoming an advocate for all and financial stability for everyone regardless of color, language or background.

Thanks for listening.

Our goal is to get this information to every student before graduating high school. Our next venture will be turning this book into a 9-week course curriculum for high schools. Contact us if you want this material in a high school near you. thebottomonup@gmail.com

www.ingramcontent.com/pod-product-compliance
Lightning Source LLC
Chambersburg PA
CBHW030001110526
44587CB00011BA/934